Insider's Guide To College Success

Insider's Guide To College Success

The Underground Playbook For Making Great Grades,
Having More Fun, and Studying Less!

DENNIS STEMMLE

College Success Academy
COLLEGE SMARTER NOT HARDER

Insider's Guide To College Success

The Underground Playbook For Making Great Grades, Having More Fun, and Studying Less!

© 2021 Dennis Stemmle

ISBN-13: 978-1-7354030-0-7 (Paperback)

This book is dedicated to:

Those students who will not let their lives be a shooting star that lights up the night sky for only a moment, but instead lives every day with real passion and purpose. For those students that choose to pursue the best version of themselves every day. For those students, better has no finish line! I admire your efforts, and I hope this book will provide encouragement and be a tool that will make your journey easier.

Praise For Insider's Guide To College Success

"A guide that can help any student in and out of the classroom. This book highlights the essential steps that are necessary to achieve your goal. After reading this book, my goals felt more achievable." - Justiss Ferraiuolo, a student at Stockton University.

"Insider's Guide to College Success answers every question an incoming college student may have. Professor Stemmle does a great job explaining how to navigate college life. This book is a must-read for all college students." - Ally Anagenesis, a student at the Monmouth University.

"This book was a great read for all college-age people. There is a lot of information in here that will be very resourceful when in college and when entering the career world." - Samantha Barrage, a student at the University of Maryland.

"Insider's Guide to College Success provides inspiration. It will encourage students to strive for their greatest potential and lead them on a path to success. A great guide for transitioning into all-important career stages. After reading this book, I feel more motivated about my upcoming transition from a county college to a university." - Ally Jensen, a student at Ocean County College.

"In this book, professor Stemmle provided me key management skills to survive in my first years of college. This is an essential read for any student aspiring for success in school or just in life." - Casey Hamilton, a student at Coastal Carolina University.

"This book is an essential guide to not only being in college but the decision to attend college and how that process starts. When you first decide to attend college, you have a lot of people with their

i

opinions and advice, but that might not always apply to you. With this book, it gives you a preview of what's to come and certain situations that might happen while in college. As a college freshman, I can say that I have experienced multiple circumstances in this book and have tried to handle them the best way I know how." - Theia Toye, a student at James Madison University.

"An informative, and first-hand insider's guide to successfully navigating the college experience. An absolute must-read for students transitioning to higher-level education, as well as current college students who are looking for tested strategies, and tools for both academic and life success." - Brandon C. Whitley, a student at Coastal Carolina University.

"I wish I had read this book before coming to college. I was not prepared for the big transition! If I would have read this before, I think it would have made an easier transition into college. This book is certainly one that I would recommend to incoming students."- Jenna Whington, a student at Coastal Carolina University.

"After giving this a read, I related with the "If you fall behind" chapter, I had hit a slump in the middle of my first semester and didn't know if or how I was going to catch up. I tried different techniques, and not much was helping, but I now realize how big it is to really talk and communicate with your professors; they want you to succeed as much as you want yourself to. I think that's a big take away from not only this book but in life." - Fred Payton, a student at Coastal Carolina University.

"This book is a great guide for students that are considering going to college. I am a college student and reading this made me want to continue my college education. College is extremely hard, and I did not have much guidance going into it. Your book gave great advice about taking notes during a lecture. I am here to say that I am one of those students that did not take notes because I would zone out. I am also the procrastinator, and honestly, that is the worst thing ever because I would turn in assignments right at the deadline." - Abria Brown, a student at Mary Baldwin University.

"Choosing a major is very difficult, and I changed it several times, and I think that was the worst thing I could have done. Although it is normal, I can agree with your ways of planning for a major." - Amani Hill-Howard, a student at Old Dominion University.

"The how-to study section in this book were beneficial and had great examples. When I was in high school, I never really studied, but when I got to college, that all had to change. The issue was I was never taught proper techniques to study, so Professor Stemmle's points were extremely helpful!" - Morgan Shell, a student at Salisbury University.

"There is a lot of pressure when having to choose a major in college, whether it is when you apply or after you have been accepted. When I was applying to college, I declared my major as undecided even though I knew I was interested in Business Management. Professor Stemmle has a lot of great points about knowing what situation is right for you on whether or not you should declare a major when applying to college. If I would have read this before applying to college, I believe I would have been more likely to applied straight into Business Management." - MacKenzie Schwartz, a student at Towson University.

"My name is Kenneth Jenkins. I attend East Carolina University in Greenville, North Carolina. I found the book "Insider's Guide To College Success" interesting. I thought that the Communicating With Your Professor section was interesting because a lot of times, students have a hard time communicating with their professors, and I liked how you suggested building relationships with professors because that is something most of us do not do, although we should. I liked how you made the book simple to understand for everyone. I didn't feel like I was reading something that was over my head at all and learned to have better communication skills with my professors from now on. I found the email guidelines beneficial as well!

I am glad I read this book because it nailed it on the head with guidelines of what to typically expect in college that will better prepare you instead of coming in with little to no knowledge." - Kelsey Wohlford, a student at Coastal Carolina University.

"This book is filled with answered questions that never seem clearly answered for high school and college students, and adults starting a career. A good read for students who strive every day to build beer versions of themselves." - Gillian Lane, a student at Ocean County College.

"All of the skills and attributes you need for a successful career are explained in-depth, which helps anyone understand how to excel in your educational goals. The perfect read for a college student who is hungry for success." - Molly Lorton, a student at Coastal Carolina University.

"In Insider's Guide to College Success, Professor Stemmle highlights many tips and tricks all college students should know. I believe it is a must-read for all incoming college students to prepare them for what is to come." - Naomi Kellmyer, a student at Coastal Carolina University.

"A really great read for all incoming college students! I wish I had seen this before I had started my undergrad career in college. These tips were very beneficial, and the book is must-read." - Joe Cariddi, a student at Stockton University.

"Professor Stemmle does a great job explaining to incoming college students what they can expect in college. His tips and tricks are very helpful, and I would recommend this book to all incoming college students." - Alexis Pastirko, a student at Rowan University.

Acknowledgments

When I first thought about writing this book, I wanted to be sure to acknowledge everybody who positively impacted my life and career. It is through others that I have gained my knowledge and experience that so powerfully contributed to me becoming the person I am today. I am eternally grateful for these mentors, coaches, and friends. This shared knowledge provided a foundation for any success I have been fortunate enough to achieve in my life.

To all the college students that provided feedback and insights on this project, I am grateful for the time you took to make this book better.

To my son Bradley who strongly encouraged me to share my thoughts and ideas with college students everywhere.

To my wife, Karen, whose support has been endless.

Finally, a thank-you to the young men and women I have had the privilege to teach over the years. May you always choose to pursue the best version of yourself!

Table Of Contents

Introduction

I am very excited you are here! You have made a great decision to invest your time and money in reading this book! This book is specifically designed to help you do college Smarter, Not Harder! This book is unique in the market! It's not another 101 tips thrown together in no specific order or sequence. This book is based not just on my personal experience but on those of hundreds of college students and professors.

Hi, I am Dennis Stemmle, college professor, bestselling author, parent of a college student, and founder of College Success Academy. As a college professor, I have seen the good, the bad, and the ugly when it comes to student performance. My goal with this book is to provide you the information you need to make your college experience a successful one.

Did you know, in the United States, we have the lowest college completion rate in the developed world? Our drop out crisis doesn't get discussed a great deal outside of education circles, but it needs to be.

The facts are alarming; Thirty percent of college freshmen don't return for their sophomore year! And surprisingly, only around half of the students who enroll in college end up graduating with a bachelor's degree!

Since 1970, undergraduate enrollment has more than doubled, but the college completion rate has been virtually unchanged. Plus, college is taking longer and longer to get through, with less than 60 percent of students who enter four-year schools finishing within six years.

And the average time-to-degree at the (so-called) four-year college hovers just over five years, with only one-third of students graduating in four years and another third taking six or more years to finish.

And the situation at community colleges is no better. Only fifty percent of students graduate within two to four years, while a full quarter of students are taking more than four years to complete their associate degree.

It's not their fault! Students and parents don't realize the challenges faced in transitioning from high school to college. The skills students learned in high school don't transfer well to the unstructured college environment. Mistakenly, students think because they did well in high school and on their ACT or SAT tests that they will do well in college, the fact is, the data just doesn't support that.

In fact, students are not only unaware of the challenges they will face in college; they are downright overconfident in their abilities.

Please head over to www.GetMyFreeBookResources.com and grab your FREE companion resources to help you get more out of this book faster!

Transitioning To College

Getting Started

An important concept that students need to understand quickly is that college is an entirely different learning system than high school. What got you to college will not make you successful in college. You need a new approach!

Let me explain; in college, the learning pyramid is flipped upside down. In high school, most of you didn't have to work too hard to be successful. You could go to class, pay attention, do some work outside of class and be simply fine. Most of your learning took place in class.

In college, you do about 20% of your learning in class and about 80% of your learning out of class. This means in college; you are going to have to spend 2-3 hours on your class requirements outside of class for each hour in which you are in the classroom. This is such a pivotal point to understand; you just can't approach college as you did in High School! In college, you must develop an entirely new approach to achieve academic success. Not only is the learning system in college completely different, how you earn your grades is different as well.

In fact, it is not unusual for 40% to 50% of your grade to be earned during the last month of the semester, which I refer to as the "The Last Month Effect." You have projects, papers, or other assignments that you are supposed to be working on all semester long. Nobody is checking in on you, asking you if you started your assignment, asking how things are going for you, etc. You are responsible for planning your assignments, looking at the due dates in the future, and creating milestones along the way to ensure you successfully complete your assignments. If you constantly wait until the last minute to tackle your assignments, as many students did in high school, it will not go well for you.

In college, you learn that you can't throw these assignments together the week before they are due and expect to make a good grade or even pass, for that matter. And if you multiply this last month effect times the four or five classes you are taking, it becomes quite easy to understand how things can unravel even for the best students.

The next big point that I want you to understand is that your GPA matters. While C's do earn degrees, and getting your college degree is an important accomplishment, one that puts you ahead of half of all students who enter college and never graduate. But did you know, a lower Grade Point Average (GPA) could sabotage your income for years? Over half of freshmen fail to realize that their GPA really does matter.

Obviously, the impact varies based on your chosen profession. But if you think just because you have chosen a career that has a set starting salary range, say like becoming a teacher, realize that the "A" students will be competing for that same job as well. A strong GPA can help you stand out from a very crowded field.

According to a recent study of compensation, a third-year financial analyst made an average total compensation of $65,000 if the person's GPA was 2.8 or less, compared to $77,000 for a GPA of 2.9 to 3.1.

The "A" student, with a GPA of 3.8 to 4.0, pulled down an average total compensation of $115,700, more than $50,000 per year premium over the 2.8 or lower graduate.

The impact of GPA is most significant early in your career, prior to you developing your work experience, a successful track record if you will. But why start behind the curve?

GPA is just so crucial to your future success, and I am going to give you the tools and information you need; not only manage your GPA and transition to college, but you will learn how to truly make your college career successful!

Things You Need To Know About College

We are told as we go off to college that we are adults now, and it's time to take 100% responsibility for our life. We probably don't give it all that much thought. I mean, what is the big deal after all?

The big deal is that this transition requires a complete mindset shift, one that moves you from passenger to driver in your life. It puts you in control; you are the cause of what's happening, not the effect of what's happening. This means that you accept that you create your life, and you are simply not reacting to what is happening to you. You appreciate that things happen for you and not to you.

One place where I pick up on the mental anchor of students is when I meet students and their parents at orientation, campus tours, and other campus events. I love these interactions, and here is what I often notice. In many cases, parents don't let their students get a word in. Other times, the student is clearly in control of the conversation. In these brief interactions, I can quickly see which student is likely to transition to college easier based on which ones have taken control of these conversations.

Taking responsibility and ownership in your life puts you in control of your choices, and this allows you to choose how to respond to the challenges college will present. You move from being a passenger in the car your parents have been driving right into the driver's seat of your college journey.

As a college professor, I hear all the excuses. I watch students place the blame on everything and everyone but themselves. They miss half of their classes, lots of assignments, and in the last week of the semester, they want their professor to make all kinds of special exceptions because of all their unique circumstances.

They send email's saying they will do whatever it takes to pass the class or raise their grades; even though they did not do the work, they want the grade.

They will blame their professors for not cutting them a break, and they play the victim card. I even had a parent one time send me an email about how hard their student worked this semester and how they were struggling to make the college transition, their maturity was not where it needed to be, and how I needed to make a special allowance for her hard-working student.

The reality was her son had not shown up to class for months. If a parent is going to be emailing a college professor, it is safe to say that student has not taken ownership of their college experience.

Even if you have taken full ownership of college and your life, procrastination is a killer for many students in college. Look, you can't wait until a few minutes or hours before an assignment is due, and then blame the dorm internet being down as a reason you could not turn your assignment in. You can't say you uploaded your assignment, but you just didn't realize the assignment was not successfully uploaded.

When you have been given an assignment and had several weeks to complete it, you can't say you locked your keys in your car at dinner and could not get your laptop until the next day when mom and dad drove to town with the second set of keys.

You can't say the rain flooded your driveway, and you could not get to your car, so you missed the test. You can't say you did not turn in the assignment because your boss made you pull a double shift or work late.

BTW these are all excuses I have heard from students. I even had a student tell me their dog ate their computer's power cord, so she could not turn in the assignment. She even had the pictures to show me.

In college, your professor must maintain the integrity of the course. They can't make individual exceptions after the fact. If you have an issue, see the professor well before the due date, and just maybe, you will be able to get an extension.

Students have told me they are missing class because they have to pick a friend up at the airport, take a friend to a court hearing, and a host of other scenarios that apparently seem reasonable to the students at the time.

I love what I heard one of my colleagues tell a student in one of these instances. He said life is all about choices! Prioritizing other tasks over your college responsibilities is a choice and one that you can make. Just accept it comes at a price, and you just can't expect a free pass.

Life is indeed all about your individual choices! The sooner you take ownership of everything in your college life, the sooner you will be on the path to college success.

Mom and Dad mean well, but things have changed quite a bit in the two or three decades that have passed since they attended college. Laptops, smartphones, tablets, social media, Netflix, Hulu, Fortnite, today's students have more distractions than any generation before.

Students are required to complete assignments, tests, sometimes even whole classes online. Your class registration, financial aid information, assignments, and grades are all accessed online. Most of your college search process, applications, and admissions process are now online, too. What worked for mom and dad just won't work for today's student.

Today's student needs to attend class more than ever before. Even if attendance is not required in your class, study after study shows there is a significant correlation between grades and class attendance. Professors work hard to help you become successful in college. Many really do take it as an insult, a sign of disrespect when you habitually miss class.

Your professors do notice who attends class and who doesn't attend their class. Do you need a letter of recommendation for a job or internship? Need some extra help with that class assignment? Need a break on a late assignment? Want the benefit of the doubt with a grade? Your attendance will be a strong influence on the outcome.

Also, many schools have mentoring programs, internships, and all kinds of other opportunities available to their high achieving students. Grades, attendance, and your extracurricular activities they all matter. Attending your classes helps you build discipline and reinforces the positive habits you need to be successful in college.

If your class is canceled, if your professor did not go over the assignment or material, guess what? Your assignment will still be due! Whether you have your class lecture or not, whether the professor mentions it, the assignments are due as assigned unless the professor explicitly changes the due date. Some professors may remind you of assignments, but most professors will not.

It is up to you to manage yourself and your coursework. Most freshman students who fail a class fail not because they could not handle the work. They fail because they didn't manage their time. They skipped classes, missed too many assignments, turned in work they threw together at the last minute, and never found time to study properly.

Don't miss assignments! Let me repeat that, DO NOT miss ANY assignments! It is extremely hard to recover from a zero in college. Even if you must turn something in of poor quality, you likely will get at least a 50. A 50 added with a 100 on your next assignment makes for a grade of a solid "C." A zero, and a 100 makes for a solid "F." So, turn something in, make your best effort! Your future self will thank you!

On university campuses across the nation, students are uttering the words, "Cs," get degrees! But don't get fooled. If you want to be successful in life, there are no "Cs," only "As" and "Fs." If you want to work for a top company, a leader in their field, you think they hire "C" students? Not too often! They hire "A" students. And guess what, once you get hired, there are only "A"s and "F"s. You either are on the team or off the team.

Look, plenty of companies hire "C" students; unfortunately, they are rarely the places you really want to work. The reason 75-80 percent of people are disengaged and dislike their jobs is strongly correlated with the compounded decisions they made for years. Don't do well in high school, you have fewer college opportunities, don't do well in college, you have fewer graduate school or job opportunities.

And on it goes. The typical student really should target a 3.5 GPA or higher. GPA matters. I don't care what you have heard! The best companies want the best students. It is that simple. Even if you are an entrepreneur in the making, investors love pedigree; they love successful students, and so do bankers!

But professor Stemmle, I want to be a teacher, and all teachers start out at the same pay regardless of GPA. That may be true, but why would they hire a "C" student to teach their kids? Why would they hire a "B" student to teach their kids? Sure, GPA will matter more in careers like finance than teaching, but if you want more opportunities, have a great GPA! Earning a high GPA requires a different approach than the one you used in high school.

In high school, students learn about 80% of the course material in class and 20% out of the classroom. In high school, many students learn if they attend class, cram the night before a test, prepare a paper or assignment a day or two before it's due, they can still make an "A" in their classes.

In high school, a bell goes off, you go to class, another bell goes off, and you go to another class, a bell goes off, you go to lunch. If you miss school, your parents get a phone call. The teachers will remind you when tests and assignments are due. It's all pretty straightforward and controlled.

Time management, discipline, organization, planning are all skills you will need to develop, foster, and embrace to be successful in college. To effectively navigate college, you will need to spend 2-3 hours outside of class for every hour in class each week! This is why it is so hard to have a job and be successful in college as a freshman or sophomore.

College really is a full-time job, and if you don't treat it as a full-time job, you will find yourself falling behind the students that do treat college as a full-time job. If you are taking a typical 15 credit hour semester, this means you should be dedicating 30-45 hours of the week to your course work while you are out of class.

Dedicating so much time to your course work is important, but students don't give much thought to how their choice of professors will impact their workload and GPA. Students may ask around a little, maybe look online at RateMyProfessors.com, but typically students are more concerned about their schedule than their professors. But not all professors are created equal.

Let's look at three different professors and see which professor you would choose?

Professor A - Has 6 Years' of experience, a lot of published articles in their field. They even have done some widely referenced industry research and wrote an acclaimed book.

Professor B – Is a newly graduated Ph.D. professor with only one semester under their belt, no published articles, no widely cited research, no books. We just don't know much about this professor.

Professor C – Has taught for 15 years, spent the last five as a dean, has come back to teaching for the last couple of years. Has a great track record of teaching, service, and contributions to the university.

Ok, who did you pick? Professor A, Professor C, few will pick Professor B. But, professor B, maybe your best choice!

I may be escorted out of the halls of every college for what I am about to tell you. Still, the reality is this is a general guideline, not a hard-fast rule, but it definitely applies more than you might think. You see, students believe they should be taking classes with long-term, accomplished tenured faculty. Each semester, I put up these professor profiles and ask students who they would like to take a class with. The overwhelming majority pick the highly experienced faculty member. But why?

On the surface, it just makes good sense. I mean, who wants to take a course with an unknown new Ph.D. graduate or a first-semester professor with only a year or two experience under their belt? But, and here is the real rub, you have to understand how the process of tenure works, how Ph.D.'s actually earn tenure, and what tenure actually means.

Let's look at how you earn tenure at most universities. The formulas change, but let's look at the most popular method. Tenure is typically earned over the course of about five years, so if a professor is a Ph.D. and teaching for over five years, they likely have tenure.

Tenure is typically earned based on three separate components: 1) Research, 2) Service to the University, 3) Teaching effectiveness, i.e., student evaluations. The hardest part of the formula for most faculty is research. Research is extremely competitive, time-consuming, and the peer review process before publishing is quite painful.

Service, that's easy; it just takes up some time. Teaching, well, here is what is beat into young Ph.D.'s across the country, don't make it hard on yourself. Good grades lead to good reviews; make it easy for your students to give you good reviews. Spend your time focusing on your research.

Now contrast this with a professor who has been teaching for over 5 years (you can bet they likely have tenure); they can't be fired unless they basically break the law or lose their academic standing. They have been overworked, likely doing two jobs for years so they can earn tenure, they are frustrated with years of student excuses, and did I mention they can't be fired unless they basically try hard to be fired!

Now from this new vantage point, which professor do you think you are more likely to have a better experience with? Which professor is likely more vested in your success? It is clear the deck is stacked in the non-tenure professors' favor.

But what about that professor who recently came back from their administration role? Don't they have a love for teaching as well?

Don't they miss the student engagement, and that is why they are back teaching? Well, maybe!

But the reality is that most university faculty can make more money in administration. The pay grades go up, and guess what, when they go back to teaching, they usually keep the same pay! What a nice way to coast into that state retirement plan.

Again, I am making broad and general statements here, and many faculty members are great, whether they are tenured or not. Still, just like in Vegas, where the odds favor the house, the odds favor the Ph.D. on the way to tenure, not already there.

But what if my professors don't have a Ph.D. or have a Ph.D. from a non-accredited school or an accredited school not recognized by my university accreditation body for tenure track? In this situation, these professors are classified as non-tenure track faculty.

Non-tenure track faculty are typically classified as either Teaching Associates who are typically full-time, or Adjunct faculty who can be full-time but typically are on a semester-to-semester renewal for their slot or position. Most Adjunct faculty are not focused on research. They are focused on teaching. They have a passion for it.

This focus on teaching often makes them very good at what they do and creates a great experience for students in the classroom. Some universities do a great job hiring Adjunct professors while others don't. It is a bit of a gamble. One thing I will say is to be careful of the Adjunct faculty member that is there to build their business.

Take, for example, the accounting professor who really doesn't care about teaching but knows it looks great for business development that they teach accounting at the university. Their teaching probably will take a back seat to their professional practice. And as a result, the student experience likely will suffer.

Retired business leaders where teaching is a second career are typically among the highest-rated faculty members at universities.

These are all general guidelines for you, and not steadfast rules. You will also gain valuable insights from other students about their individual experiences with professors. One benefit students receive from joining university clubs or organizations is access to students who have already gone down the road you are going. Their insights can be unbelievably valuable.

Of course, you can always check out RateMyProfessor.com and other online sources as the last result.

Another important habit to get into is to pay close attention to your professor's introduction about themselves on the first day of class! Do they seem excited, enthusiastic, or are they just going through the motions?

Avoid Making Excuses

Your college professor doesn't want to hear about how hard you worked, how much effort you put in, how you suffer from test anxiety, how you didn't sleep well the night before, or what a difficult time you are going through due to a breakup, a job loss, or what have you.

It is not that they don't care or that they don't want you to be successful. It's they have 100's of students, they can't make all these judgment calls, so they have to rely on university-approved absence guidelines, syllabus requirements, and such to ensure fair and equitable treatment to all students.

Look, everybody responds to life events differently. I know students who lost a grandparent and missed a month of class, had to make a semester withdrawal and others who were back in class the same or next day. Most universities are not self-paced, and as such, you are responsible for delivering your work in accordance with university and class guidelines.

In college and in life, you get rewarded for your results, not your effort, whether you are going through a difficult time or are on cloud nine. So, what if something did happen and your performance was, let's say, below your standard.

Many professors will allow students to drop their lowest test or assignment grade; some will even replace a grade with an exam grade, some will allow extra credit. The best course of action is to actually make sure the rest of your class work is your best work. Demonstrate that the one assignment, test, quiz, etc., was an outlier. Remember the importance of attending class? It all comes back to showing the professor you really did just have an unusual situation impacting your grade. Professors are human. They understand things happen. Some will adjust your grade; some will not. Either way, you have stepped up and done your best to recover.

Most of the students who come to me at the end of the semester have demonstrated a subpar performance all semester. The fact is, poor performance is a simple output resulting from poor discipline and habits. There is a lot you can do to recover from setbacks early in the semester; not much can be done in the last couple of weeks. If you have an issue, talk to your professor immediately, don't worry about being embarrassed; they have likely heard your story before. Waiting until 80-90 percent of your grade is complete to have the conversation leaves no time to course correct.

In high school, you could memorize some facts the night before the exam, ace the test, and forget what you knew two days later. This is an example of memorizing, and memorizing is not learning. In college, you most often need to learn, not memorize. You will be given various different scenarios designed to test that you actually understand the underlying ideas and concepts of their interaction and the impact of the different concepts, and how they may influence each other. In college, you just can't memorize a bunch of formulas and not understand what those formulas are designed to achieve. You will have to develop a deep understanding of the concepts so you will know what formulas to apply to the problem at hand.

Many students who were successful in math in high school struggle with math in college, and they can't figure out why. Their struggles typically result from the student not developing a deep enough understanding of the concepts; they get the formulas, the math. Still, they struggle to apply them in the correct manner. Memorizing something results in you knowing something; learning something results in your understanding something, and these two concepts couldn't be more different.

Memorizing implies that there is only one right answer for each question we are asked. Understanding sees multiple answers to each question. Memorizing something simply allows you to solve problems when the components or numbers are presented the same each time. Understanding something allows you to calculate the right answer as the individual variables change. Success in college requires you to focus on learning and understanding, not memorizing.

You Have to Do the Work

Everybody wants to be successful, but few students want to do what is necessary to become successful. About half of all the students who enter college, never graduate. Thirty percent of freshmen don't return for the Sophomore year. If you get through your first couple of semesters, you have significantly increased your odds of success.

I am a believer that everyone who gets into college is smart enough to handle the course work. Most of the students who don't succeed in college, lack the habits, focus, and discipline needed to succeed. The other big reason students don't graduate is that college is expensive.

16

Poor performance can lead to lost scholarships, lost parental support, and so on.

All across the country, as the semester comes to an end, students are losing scholarships, financial aid, athletic eligibility, and what have you. Students panic and start reaching out to professors to allow them to make things up, as they can't afford to lose their scholarship, they can't lose their eligibility, they can't go back home as there is nothing good for them there, and so on and so on. They say they will do whatever they need to do; just please give them an opportunity! They want the professors to provide them with a free pass based on their individual circumstances, and life doesn't work that way. You can't miss half your classes, a bunch of your assignments, and then when it comes time to pay the price for your actions, expect your professor to pay the price for you. Life doesn't work that way!

Make sure you do the work! Develop winning habits and focus on getting great results out of the gate. Getting off to a quick start in college is key to your college success, and quite honestly, success in life.

The Summer Before College

The summer before college is an exciting time in a student's life, but it is also can be a pretty stressful time as well. If you're in a relationship, you are likely stressed about if that relationship will continue; if you try to date across the miles, you might be concerned if the relationship will last. You are wondering if you will get along with your new roommates, just how much you will miss your friends, how hard it will be to make new friends, and will you get homesick. On top of all this, I know many students are working hard to save a little more money before they leave for college, while others are trying to squeeze as much time with friends and family that they can before they head off to college.

But regardless of your personal situation, I want to make sure your transition to campus life is as smooth as possible. And if you are already on campus, already struggling, I am going to cover all the things you must do in order to be successful in college and make your time in college as stress-free as possible. But before we get started, I want to make sure those students heading off to college get the most out of their college orientation.

I highly recommend you schedule your college orientation session as early as possible. At most universities, you will sign up for your classes during orientation, and as they say, the early bird gets the worm, and when it comes to college, that means getting in the best classes and having an optimal schedule. I know this is not what the university will tell you, and yes, most universities do set aside the same number of slots for students in classes regardless of the orientation session, but here is the rub, most universities can't balance the slots for 8:00 a.m. classes versus the 5:00 p.m. classes, MWF classes versus TTH classes which are more driven by faculty schedules then supply and demand, so it really is first come first serve. I can tell you most students' class schedule sweet spot is from 9:00 a.m. to Noon. Most students struggle with 8:00 a.m. classes and late afternoon and evening classes.

During orientation, you also will get your student ids, sign up for your meal plan, and learn your required course books and materials. Class materials can be expensive, so you might want to do some price shopping online. During orientation, you can get your book list and determine which books you will get at the campus bookstore and which ones you can find cheaper online. When making your price comparisons keep in mind that used books usually don't come with online access codes that may be required for your class to complete assignments and quizzes, so make sure you are comparing apples to apples. By getting your books early, you can read a few chapters in each of your textbooks prior to arriving on campus and develop a solid foundation for your initial class lectures.

Another great thing about college orientation is you will be able to see your dorm, meet your RA, and get an idea of just how small the space is you will have to live and work in. Another important thing to accomplish during orientation is to check into transferring any of your medical prescriptions, seeing a doctor on and off campus, learning about your campus health care options, and any other personal needs you may have.

Orientation is also a great time to find out about your tech needs on campus. I typically advise you stick with a PC, not a Mac. I love Apple products, but Apple products often don't play well with Moodle and other university tech platforms. Most professors will require you to upload your documents in Word, Excel, or PDF. Yes, you can convert your Apple files, but I can tell you every semester, somebody forgets and uploads a file that can't be read. When this happens, your professor has no idea what you actually uploaded, so guess what, you just earned a zero.

You might also have some issues taking your online tests, quizzes, and exams. Check with the university staff and professors during orientation, and they will point you in the right tech direction. Also, you will want to join your graduating class social media group. These groups are a great way for you to connect and ask questions of other students. Parent groups are generally available as well, allowing mom and dad to communicate with other parents.

How do you register for classes? How do you check your grades, submit assignments, and check assignment due dates? Universities use platforms like WebAdvisor to manage their class registrations, class drops, class adds, class grades, financial aid, and a host of other things. Additionally, most universities will use Learning Management Systems like Moodle and Blackboard to manage student classes and assignments. These university LMS will allow you to manage your classes, schedules, assignments, and your university student account in one place.

It is important for you to realize that each of your professor will manage their classes differently, but a well laid out LMS is a strong indication that your professor is on top of things.

Some professors will actually have an assignment due the first day of class; maybe it is a book to read, a case study, or what have you. Many students will not have a clue that they were supposed to do an assignment before they get to campus and start day one in the hole. Additionally, many of your classes will likely have an online component based on your class text. Two of the more popular textbook providers are McGraw Hill and Pearson. Both companies offer students a free two-week trial, but if you don't purchase the book and or online access code during the trial period, your work will be lost.

In college, you will be doing a lot of writing, so you will want to purchase grammar software. My favorite software is Grammarly. Grammarly automatically detects grammar, spelling, punctuation, word choice, and style mistakes in your writing. Without it, you will be at a competitive disadvantage in the writing of your papers and assignments.

Additionally, your school will likely have several apps for you to download. These typically give you campus maps, shuttle schedules, general and emergency information, and updates and alerts about campus activities. Learning to navigate all these different systems will take some time, so the earlier you start the process, the better.

The Core Will Drive Your First Two Years

Typically, your first two years of college are focused on your core requirements. Regardless of your major, each state university will have a core curriculum. The core is made up of the basic courses that are going to be required regardless of your major. Many of your core courses will require you to pass with a "C" or better. Because there is such a wide range of classes that you can take to meet your core requirements, you really want to get familiar with all your options.

If you have made a decision on your major or if you have narrowed your choice down, you can ask for a copy of each major's 4-year plan. The requirements for some university majors like the STEM majors will require you to focus more on the technical and quantitative type of courses. Management and Marketing may require one math, while finance and accounting may require a more advanced math class.

You want to pay close attention to the foundational courses that are prerequisites for your more advanced classes. You want to get these courses out of the way as soon as possible so that you create flexibility in your scheduling. Some universities only teach certain classes in the Fall, and if you miss that class, you are now stuck in summer school, or you just added another semester to your time in school.

Figuring Out Dining

Meal plans usually are the best way to go your first year on campus. Dining halls are usually well placed on campus and offer a wide variety of foods regardless of their dietary needs. They are also super convenient and help ensure students are more likely to eat and eat a well-balanced meal. You will be able to purchase a meal plan during orientation. As an FYI, often, the food on campus is upgraded during orientation sessions. Some students report that they feel like their university meal plan quality drops significantly compared to what was available during orientation, so it might be worth asking around while you are on campus.

University meal plans typically will have money available to eat at the restaurant chains on campus, Chick-fil-A, Panera, Starbucks, etc. Dorm floors are not set up well for preparing your own meals, and the common area can be a free for all. Meal plans are usually sold as an unlimited use plan or with a specific number of meals. If you buy the whole year in advance, you will save a good bit of money, but if you transfer or drop out after the first semester, these meal plans are typically not refundable.

Typically, when students move off campus, they drop the meal plans, but many students get frustrated with their roommates eating their food, not cooking on their assigned days, etc., so they go back to their campus meal plan.

Get Organized

You want to get your planner early so you can start to manage all your activities. I go into all the details in the time management chapter, but for now, you want to identify the dates for move-in, class start dates, and any mandatory student training like substance abuse, safety on campus, etc., that you may be required to take prior to classes starting.

One of the first big events on campus is parents' weekend, and hotels will fill up fast, so you may want to have your parents book their parent's weekend hotels during orientation; then again, you might not want to do that! Just saying! You want to check the dates for your fall break or spring break, based on when you are starting college. Flights get really expensive over breaks, so booking ahead of time can save you a bundle.

You also want to quickly identify the drop/add date for your classes. These are the few days; you have to drop a class and add another class with no issues. There is a host of reasons you may end up dropping a class. You might quickly realize you can't understand half the words coming out of your calculus professors mouth due to her thick accent, a class that was full may now have an opening, you may not like the professor once you met them, whatever the reason, it is important to realize the drop/add time window is short, typically just a few days.

During orientation is a great time to see where your classes are. You can check out the lecture halls or classrooms and see how big or how small the rooms are.

I recommend you actually walk the path you will take to class and time how long it takes, especially if you are on a large campus. If you have to take a shuttle, make sure you know how many stops your shuttle will make. Find the library, the fitness center, the writing lab, the dining halls, and restaurants.

If your university doesn't have a pharmacy or health center, you will want to identify a doctor and a pharmacy close to your campus. Identify the local big box stores, grocery stores, coffee shops, etc. If you are bringing a car to college, you want to identify which parking lots are assigned to your dorm. If you are driving to any of your classes, you will need to know where your student parking is located relative to your classes. On most campuses, parking is a nightmare; you will need to leave ample time to find a place to park.

You will also want to check out the student union, as most colleges have daily activities going on and lots of free entertainment options, plus it is a great place to meet other students.

During orientation, colleges typically have an area where you can go check out the clubs and organizations available to you on campus. These events provide you the opportunity to meet other students with common interests. Typically, in your first-year experience class, you will be required to check out a specific number of clubs and join a club or two. Most universities will have a club and organization day, so you can check out many opportunities in a short period of time.

Connecting with folks on campus will help you transition to college quicker; it will make you feel like a part of the community and reduce the homesickness you may experience. Grades are important, but having fun is also essential, and university clubs and organizations are a great way to create balance in your life.

Most universities have all their student clubs and organizations listed on their website, so spend a little time taking a look at all your options before you even get to campus.

Universities typically will get you set up with your school email account shortly after your acceptance. As I previously mentioned, universities use LMS like MOODLE to manage most of your course work, and you may have an assignment due on your first day of class, so log into your account and check for any summer reading or other assignments often!

Modeling Success

Congratulations! You made your college decisions, and you are excited to get started on the next chapter of your life. Not to derail your enthusiasm, but the real work is just about to begin.

In this section, I am going to look at the things successful students do, so you can model them, learn from them, and avoid the costly trial and error process that leaves half of the students failing to figure things out, failing to graduate. I don't want that to happen to you; I don't only want you to graduate, I want you to graduate with a high GPA, I want you to graduate with a clear vision for your life, I want you to graduate with that dream job all lined up!

If you're like the majority of students entering college, you are excited to start this next phase of your life, but you probably don't have a clear vision for your life. You probably are uncertain about the career you want to pursue, and even the major you are going to select, and that is ok.

Many students pick a major based on their desire to make a good living, earn a good income, and be successful, or maybe their parents do a certain thing, so they think, "why not try what mom or dad does."

Students stress out about picking a major, and most universities give you your first two years to figure it all out. Let me let you in on a big secret; most people don't end up working in a job closely related to their major. A recent study showed that only 27% of people were working in a job closely related to their major. 27%! But my guess would be that well over 90% of students stress about picking their major! Some 30% of students end up not just changing majors but transferring universities as well.

Look, college is hard work, and having a vision for your life will provide you with the motivational foundation you will need to do the hard work. A clear vision for your life helps connect the dots, helps push you to do all the hard work ahead.

Sallie has always wanted to be an Accountant! She loves numbers, and she wants to help small business owners grow their businesses. Growing up, she saw the negative impacts of not understating your numbers when her family's company went bankrupt; She saw the stress and frustration that created. She vowed to help other families avoid that same fate. She knows she needs her CPA to make that happen. And she knows she needs a Master's in Accounting to sit for the CPA exam in her state. She also knows she needs a good GPA in college to get into graduate school. You think Sallie will be motivated to do the hard work? You bet she will! She has a clear vision of where she wants to go. Her vision is like a magnet, pulling her in the direction of her dreams. Unfortunately, only about one in ten students have this kind of focused vision.

Most students are more like Bill. Bill is not sure what he wants to do in the future. He has heard from his parents, teachers, and coaches, that if he wants to be successful, he needs to go to college. He likes the idea of a business major because he figures that businesses are everywhere and majoring in business will give him a lot of options.

His parents are pushing him to find his path, so he decides he will pick management as a major so he can quickly answer the "what's your major" questions. He's had enough of dealing with all the lectures from well-meaning adults about how important picking your major is.

Bill figures that everybody needs to hire managers, so why not choose management, and off he goes to start his new life. But here is the problem, your first two years of college look a lot like high school, with a big focus on your core curriculum requirements. Bill can't figure out why he needs the English, Math, and History courses he is taking. He thought college would be different. Not only does he not know why he is taking these classes, he has no desire to write the papers, take the tests, and study so hard for a bunch of stuff he sees no use in!

Who do you think is more likely to have a successful semester, Sallie, or Bill? My money would be on Sallie. These two student examples demonstrate the importance of having a vision for your life. If you want to be successful in college and life, you have to develop a vision for what you want to accomplish in your life. But don't worry, that is a big part of what college is all about. You have four-plus years to figure out what kind of person you want to be, what kind of life you want to lead.

Once you are sure about who you are and what you want, it's easy to psych yourself up to achieve your goals. If you're not sure, it's nearly impossible. It is very essential that you start to live your life with intention!

Most people float through life, waiting for things to happen to them. A study conducted by a prominent psychologist found that 94% of people had no purpose for their lives, 94 percent! They are like leaves blowing in the wind, going wherever the wind takes them. I don't want your life to be like a leaf blowing in the wind.

I'll make it simple; if you don't have a vision yet, you must have a specific daily goal. A goal that moves you toward becoming the best version of yourself. The key is to create positive momentum.

No idea what you want to do when you graduate? Then your vision should likely be to ensure you graduate, be the best student you can be while you actively seek new experiences to help you figure it all out. But here is what happens all too often.

Let's look at John. John is a junior, and he just got to take his first investment class, and he fell in love with investing. He wants to become an investment manager and knows that getting a job on wall street is where he wants to be. Here is the problem, John didn't take his course work conscientiously in his first two years. He knew C's get degrees, and he figured just graduating would place him ahead of 50% of his colleagues who don't.

Now he has found his vision, his passion, but with a 2.1 GPA, there is not much chance any big Wall Street firm will hire him. He knows he has some time left before graduating, but even if he makes a perfect 4.0 GPA in his last two years, he will just break the 3.0 bar. He now knows what he wants to do, but by not doing his best work in his first two years of college, he is now extremely frustrated and angry with himself. He now realizes he will have to go to graduate school and try to be able to demonstrate he is the kind of student the big wall street firms will want to hire.

Now your goals will probably be different than Johns, but regardless of your goals, the principles and approaches are what matter. Set your sights high each semester and challenge yourself. Have an extremely specific GPA goal. About half of the students have a goal of just doing their best. This is a terrible goal; it lets you off the hook way too easily; it doesn't provide you a clear, specific, and measurable goal to pursue. Set your sight's on making the Dean's List, having a 3.5 GPA, 3.7 GPA, 4.0 GPA, or whatever goal will stretch you.

You will not figure out your vision for your life by doing the same things over and over every day, staying in your comfort zone. You will find your vision, your passion, by seeking new experiences, meeting new people, asking lots of questions, and focusing on the process.

Let's look at two students. Jordan is in business school, but she is not sure what she wants to major in. She decides she wants to join a few clubs and gain some new experiences. She is not quite sure what direction she wants to take, so she decides that joining the marketing club and the accounting club will give her two separate points of view. She also joins a sorority because she values the social experience college offers. Her organization has a big fundraiser coming up, and she decides she will volunteer to manage the marketing for the event. She has learned a few marketing ideas in her marketing club that she thought would work well. Jordan goes to work utilizing social media, hosting info events all over campus, and discovers she loves planning these info events. She loves the interaction with people; she enjoys planning and organizing things. She decides she wants to host live events for a living. She decides to pursue her new vision for her life and decides to pursue a double major in marketing and event management.

Zach decides he doesn't want to get involved in campus activities yet. He wants to hang out with his best friend Steve from high school, as they are now college roommates. They are taking all the same classes. They are looking forward to life without their parents standing over them, telling them what to do. They love playing video games, hanging out, and chilling. Zach is enjoying his newfound freedom and independence. He goes to class, studies, is doing fine with his grades, but he can't figure out why he still doesn't know what he wants to do. He is even starting to question if college is even for him.

By creating new experiences, Jordan found her vision. Zach is stuck in a routine, a comfort zone. He has not pushed himself to discover new things, try new experiences, meet new people with different perspectives and views. He is still lost in his comfort zone.

Even if you get out of your comfort zone, the place where students and most people fail in life is that they don't maintain the discipline to execute every day. Lack of daily execution toward a goal is notably lacking when students are uncertain about their future, unsure about their majors, unsure about their future careers.

Google discipline, and you will find it defined one way, but here is how I define it: Here is something I know that I am supposed to do that I don't want to do. Can you make yourself do it? Can you make yourself do It!

I think everybody can relate to this definition because most of us have demonstrated a lack discipline several times each day, week, or month. Here is something that I know I am supposed to do that I don't want to do. Can you make yourself do it? And over here, there is something that you know you are not supposed to do, but you want to do it. Can you keep yourself from doing it?

We all make these seemingly innocent choices and decisions every day. A success mindset is what helps us to stay focused on the process of what we need to do to accomplish the vision that we have for our lives.

Do I stay in bed or go to class? Do I stay home and study for my exam or go out and party with my roommates? Do I complete the assignment today or push it off to another time when I feel like it?

It is not hard to figure out, but it is hard to implement in our lives. Here is a simple example: I want to lose 15 pounds; that's my goal. Plenty of programs have clearly defined everything that I am supposed to do to achieve that goal. Where do we fail? Why, after two or three days, are we back to eating cookies and ice cream?

Discipline is a tremendous battle for everybody! How many times have you heard somebody say, I don't feel like doing that? Here is a hard truth, a harsh reality, it doesn't matter what you feel like! Let me say that again; it doesn't matter what you feel like! You have to make choices and decisions based on what you want to accomplish.

You have to be committed to it, and it has to be important to you for you to able to do it. Not because your parents said it was a good idea, not because a professor told you to do it, do it because it is important to you!

Once you have a vision, once you commit to doing what you need to do, you have to figure out what sacrifices you are willing to make? You are going to have to set priorities.

You are certainly going to have to make some sacrifices if you want to accomplish anything significant in your life. What knowledge are you going to have to acquire? What classes are you going to have to take to be able to acquire that knowledge? What obstacles are you going to have to overcome on your journey?

You need to control your priorities, and you will have to develop the discipline to stay focused on those priorities. Are you able to focus on the vision that you have, or are you going to be affected by the circumstances that you are in all the time?

Let me tell you a story. When Ulysses S. Grant took over the Union Army, President Lincoln expected him to ask for things that Lincoln could not deliver, as had the other commanders of the Union Army had done before him. There were15,000 troops near Harpers Ferry with no horses. The prior commanders had focused on getting more horses, but there were no horses to be found. Lincoln expected Grant to make the same impossible request.

As Lincoln expected, Grant wanted to talk about those men near Harpers Ferry with no horses, but to his surprise, he did not ask for horses; he asked if he could convert those troops to infantry or release them from their duties.

Grant definitely had a success mindset! Lincoln said, "He didn't ask impossibilities of me, and he's the first general I have had that didn't, in designing his plans and strategies." Grant understood that resources are finite. Accepting this fact is the first step in setting a realistic plan.

Successful students understand their strengths and weaknesses, they put in the time to make sure they are prepared. They develop their plans based on their reality, not their parents, not their roommates, not other students.

If you allow other's expectations to dominate your thoughts, those expectations can affect you because it makes it much more difficult for you to stay focused on your plan, the process of things because you are so worried about letting others down.

So, you need to be focused on something extendable daily; not how many test you ace, not how many honors you achieve, it needs to be focused more towards what actions do I have to take that support my plan and will allow me to achieve my goals and vision for my life.

The foundation for forming good success habits starts with a clear understanding of your goals and the development of an effective time management system.

At first, you will feel like you have more time available to you than you will know what to do with. Even if you take a huge class load, have a part-time job, and sleep a lot, I guarantee that initially, you are going to feel like you have more time than you imagined.

This feeling is all a grand illusion and is the underlying reason why most students find themselves overwhelmed, depressed, and having to pull the dreaded all-nighters that everybody fears.

You see, in college, it is not unusual for 40% to 50% of your grade to be earned in the last month of a semester. While you are cruising along with little care at the start of the semester, that last month is out there looming, waiting to reap havoc on your GPA. This last month is like a mountain that has accumulated snow over the winter months; a slight change in conditions can bring about an avalanche. What seemed like a manageable workload has now spun out of control. The avalanche is upon you.

Time management makes all the difference in succeeding in college, graduating on schedule, enjoying this time in your life, or completely struggling and being stressed out, and maybe, like 50% of students who enter college, completely dropping out altogether. As such, I wrote a whole book on this topic, "Time Management Secrets For College Students," and I dedicate an entire chapter to Time Management in this book.

Expect to be Challenged

If you expect everything to be easy, if you expect everything to work out well, everything to be a straight line to success, you are going to be greatly disappointed. Because it's never going to happen that way.

If your expectation is that things are going to be difficult, that there are going to be challenges and setbacks, and you look at those challenges as opportunities to grow and develop to accomplish something of significance, then you are going have a much better chance to keep the kind of positive attitude about things you need to execute your plan and achieve your goals.

According to research conducted by social psychologist Dr. David McClelland of Harvard, the people you consistently associate with will determine as much as 95 percent of your success or failure in life.

This is why it is so important to hang out with other success-minded students, students that have a vision for their future, or students who are working hard to achieve their dreams. If you are interested in Marketing, join the American Marketing Association on campus, hang around other students that are going on the same journey. Interested in Marine Science? Join the marine science group on campus. In most cases, you will not be able to take any courses in your major in your first semester on campus, but you can join the student groups associated with your desired major or possible majors. You can talk to upper-classmen and get their insights and mentorship. You can spark your interest in a field or figure out if it might be time to try something new.

Many students have a real hard time leaving behind some of their negative influences from high school. Nothing will derail your college career faster than hanging out with a bunch of students focused on the wrong things. The students that are out partying every night are unmotivated to do their coursework. They are basically looking to do anything but their schoolwork. They are embracing their new freedom, are focused on enjoying the moment, and have no real plan for their future!

There is strong research that indicates you are the average of the five people you spend the most time with. The people that you spend your time with shape who you are and who you become. These people will determine what conversations and thoughts control your attention. They affect the attitudes and behaviors you are repeatedly exposed to. Eventually, you start to think as they think and behave as they behave. Make sure you hang out with success-minded students, and you are well on your way to college success.

Nutrition Matters

If you're like a lot of people, you skip a healthy breakfast before class; then, you will hit a vending machine between classes because you are hungry and tired. You grab your lunch on the go or skip it altogether. You come home from classes after a long day, and you will throw a pizza in the microwave, maybe down something from the university vending machines, or perhaps you'll grab a latte and scone. You decide to skip your workout again, you are downing those energy drinks, so you are not sleeping well, you are getting stressed out from your course workload, and your well-being is suffering. Successful students stay hydrated, get plenty of sleep, exercise, and eat a balanced diet.

Successful Students Know Themselves

They don't plan on studying on Saturday at 8:00 a.m., when they know they will be out on Friday night, into the early hours of Saturday morning. It is fine to go out and have a good time, which is an important part of the college experience. But skipping an important assignment to go out, telling yourself you can throw that paper together in an hour or two before the deadline, and you will be fine, well then, you're just kidding yourself. That approach might have worked fine in high school, but it won't work well in college.

High Standards Are Important

You have to create a high standard for your work, for your effort, and for your character. You want to set a high standard, a standard people can believe in, people can count on! The people who routinely achieve the most in this world maintain incredibly high standards for themselves and those around them.

People with high standards believe that everything matters, big or small, it all matters. Regardless of the importance of the activity, they take pride in their work. They believe everything they do is all a reflection of who they are, what they represent.

They hold themselves to the highest standards because they know that without a high standard, they will not achieve what they want to achieve and become the people they want to be. They treat every assignment as important; they do every assignment to the best of their ability.

I am reminded of a story I heard as a kid; I can't recall the baseball players' names, but I remember the story very well, and it has helped shaped my character. It was late in the game, and the team was well out of it; everybody was in a hurry to just get the heck out of there.

This player who had a high standard for himself aggressively ran down a fly ball, diving for it and making an amazing catch. After the game, another player asked him why he did that, why he risked injury for a play that didn't matter.

His response was an insightful look into his character. He said every play mattered and that there were fans in the stadium that day who had paid good money to be there, fans that supported his salary, the team, and his future, and some fans might even be seeing him play for the first time, he was never going to show those people anything but his best.

If you want to be successful, want to separate yourself from the pack, start by raising the standards for yourself. Start by not accepting anything but your best in everything you do.

Part 2:
Academic Skills

Classroom Skills

Properly utilizing your classroom time is critical to your success in college. In college, you do the majority of your learning outside the classroom. Making the most of your class time will reduce the work you have to do out of the classroom. Don't waste that class time, don't goof off on social media, don't chat with your classmate sitting next to you, don't get distracted thinking about all the things you have to do later, and by all means, don't try to catch up on some sleep.

Being prepared for class is a challenge for all students, not just for college freshmen. To be prepared, you must first actually understand what it takes to be properly prepared for each individual class.

The truth of the matter is, what is properly prepared for one class is actually quite different than being prepared for another class. And preparation will vary by each student's strengths and weaknesses. The prep work for your first-year experience class will be much different than the prep work for your math class or even your English 201 class.

For most students, STEM classes require the most prep work. Let's take math as an example. To properly prepare for your math class, you need to do a few things. First, you need to read the applicable chapters, watch the applicable videos, or review whatever prep material the professor has provided prior to the class lecture.

Second, you need to work on the practice questions prior to class. And finally, you should prepare questions for class based on where you are struggling. This is all very crucial to your overall success.

Look, most high school students don't need to do this in their high school classes, but in most college STEM classes, you will have a lot more coming at you at a much faster pace. If you get lost early, which will happen if you don't prepare, you will be lost for the whole lecture.

With preparation, you won't know how to ask a question or describe to the professor why or where you are lost. All that you will know is that you don't get it.

Your prep work is meant to identify areas where you need help, where you need to pay close attention, where you will need to ask your questions to ensure you leave the classroom with a clear understanding of the course material. Sometimes you may not be able to ask questions, sometimes the professor will clear things up for you during the lecture, but many times you will need to head to the tutoring center. Don't allow yourself to get behind. Seek help immediately, go to the tutoring center early and often. The tutoring center should be used to prepare, don't wait to go to the tutoring center or seek help after you have performed poorly on a test or assignment. Successful students use the tutoring center as part of their preparation.

If you are still struggling, go see your professor or the teaching associate (TA). When it comes to exam time, make the exam review a priority! Never skip an exam review. These reviews are critical to helping you understand where to focus your study efforts.

With math classes, studies show you should work at least three sets of exam problems around each key topic. It is no secret, many college professors teach right out of the class text. They cover just the material in the book and interject little additional information into their class lectures. For those classes, you might find you just need to show up to class and take good notes with little or no prep work, but I encourage you to err on the side of over preparation and then scale back as you learn your professor's approach and gain experience with understanding your strengths and weaknesses.

Muhammad Ali said - "The fight is won or lost far away from the witnesses, behind the lines, in the gym, and out there on the road; long before I dance under those lights." and the same is true for college success!

A boxer would not think about entering the ring without doing the prep work. A football team doesn't enter a game without watching the film on their opponent and developing a game plan! So, why would you enter a college classroom unprepared, not having done your prep work!

Stay Focused

Being in class doesn't mean just showing up and filling a seat. It means actively listening, being engaged in dialog, asking questions, and taking ownership of your education.

Stay off your phone, stay off your computer and take notes with a pen or pencil. Studies show that handwriting your notes is some 30% more effective than utilizing your computer.

Look, you're only in your class for about an hour. Find a way to stay disconnected from your devices and stay connected to your lecture. Staying focused is not easy; you must work on your active listening skills. If you don't develop your abilities to concentrate, to actively listen in college, you will pay the price not just in college but in your career as well.

If you think your class lecture is boring, wait until you sit in your corporate meetings when you land that first job. You must learn to improve your concentration and focus on being successful in college, your career, and your life.

Prepping for class, actively engaging in class puts you well down the path to college success and success in life as well!

A big part of prepping for a class is understanding how your body language impacts things. Your body language not only impacts your professors' perceptions of you as a student, but it actually impacts how you feel and perform.

What is body language? It is a non-verbal communication method that includes your specific facial expressions, the tone of your voice, eye contact, body posture and motions, and positioning within groups. It can also include things like the way we wear our clothes or the silence we keep.

As much as 93 % of our communication is not actually the words we use!

- 7% of what we communicate is in our words.
- 38% of what we communicate is actually a result of our voice inflections and cadence.
- 55% of our communication is based on the nonverbals we are showing.

We don't realize that other people are significantly influenced by our nonverbals, and not only that, but we ourselves are also influenced by our nonverbals, our thoughts, and our feelings, and our physiology.

Research in recent years has revealed something strange. We have learned that our bodies not only express our minds, but the body directly influences the mind in its own way.

It turns out, our experiences are part of our thinking. This research is part of a developing field in psychology known as embodied cognition, whose main thesis is that our bodies and the world around us not only influence us but are intimately woven within our thoughts.

Studies within this field have discovered some very interesting results. Take, for example, the act of sitting; it turns out that sitting in a hard chair makes people less willing to compromise. Need to get your way? Make sure the person you are negotiating with is sitting in a comfortable chair. Holding a heavy clipboard caused people to take their work more seriously; holding a warm drink made people judge another as more generous and caring than those holding cold drinks.

41

A study from San Francisco State University found that slouching can cause you to feel sad and depleted of energy. The study also discovered that changing your posture to an upright position can cause an improvement in mood and energy.

Frustrated, feel like quitting? Try crossing your arms. Studies have shown that crossing our arms has shown to make people more persistent and willing to work longer on difficult problems.

Are you feeling down? Just smile. The act of smiling can pick you up out of a negative mood and lower your overall stress levels. While sticking with crumpled eyebrows and negative expressions causes you to see the world in a more cynical light.

Ok, so you understand the importance of preparing for class, paying attention to your body language, and actively engaging in class, but did you know where you sit can significantly impact your GPA? In class, you are going to want to sit upfront.

Studies show that students that sit in the back average a full letter grade below students that sit in the front. Sitting up front forces you to concentrate, pay attention, and engage. Students who sit in the front are naturally more engaged. I rarely see an "A" student sitting in the back of the class.

No matter how well you prepare, how well you engage, you will, at times, have gaps between what you know and what you need to know. What you think you know and what you actually know. This is not just true in college, but in life as well.

Your job in the classroom is to make sure you clearly identify any gaps you have during each lecture. Then during your planning process, you need to develop a plan to fill in those gaps well ahead of your exam date. For example, will you need multiple tutor sessions, visits to your professor or teaching associate? Will you need to watch a few hours of YouTube videos, attend group study sessions, or what have you?

The execution of your plan needs to make it into your planner. The steps you need to take to fill in the gaps have to be scheduled to ensure they actually happen. This allows you to get the most out of your study time.

Studying Should be About Reviewing, Not Learning!

The reason students get stuck pulling all-nighters is simple, they didn't prepare, they procrastinated, and they are still trying to learn the material. If you treat your college experience like a job, you will be successful. If you try to fly by the seat of your pants, you are going to crash.

Treat college like a full-time job from day one, and you will avoid a lot of the pain and suffering most students endure. Step up your game, do the work, and you will succeed. One way to get the most out of all your hard work is to schedule your classes to your body's natural rhythms and sleep cycles. Don't schedule an 8:00 a.m. class if you will sleep through half that class! If you typically crash after 3:00 p.m., don't schedule evening classes. If you are a morning person, schedule classes early. If you are more of a night owl, schedule your classes accordingly.

If you are going to be out late every Monday night, don't schedule an 8:00 a.m. Tuesday class. "But professor Stemmle, I don't have a choice; the only time I can take the class I need is at 8:00 a.m." Well, there might just be a way around that.

Ok, so here is an inside tip for you. Go to the class section you have been assigned, sit up front, and be engaged. Go by and meet your professor during office hours to discuss what it takes to be successful in their class, talk about your major, talk about how they got into teaching, it doesn't matter what you talk about, you just want to build a good relationship.

Around week three of the semester, things will have settled down, and you can approach your professor. You can say something like, my sorority sister is in your 9:25 am Tuesday, Thursday class, and she mentioned there were several open seats. Is it ok if I attend your 9:25 a.m. class instead of the 8:00 a.m. class?

The key here is you are asking to attend, not transfer sections; you just want to attend the class at a different time. If there are open seats, and the professor knows who you are, they will very likely let you attend a class you are not assigned to.

If you can truly say something meaningful, like my roommate is in your 9:25 a.m., and it would help a lot if you could commute in together, or my work schedule changed, and I am getting home much later than I anticipated and the extra hour sleep would allow you to engage in the class in a more effective manner, your professor may take pity on you.

Some professors will be like, life is full of choices, you need to decide what is more important, etc., but many professors are happy to accommodate students when than can. Make sure you make this request in private, and make sure you let your professor know it is not something you will mention to other students.

Take Great Lecture Notes

Taking good lecture notes is another critical skill you need to develop as a college student. In fact, only about 10% - 15% of college students actually know how to take good notes. I want you to be one of those few students that actually know how to take great notes, so let's take a look at how you can be among those select few.

The first key to good notetaking is to understand that less is not more. You should be writing during most of your class lecture time. You want to make sure you not only capture the key ideas but the supporting lecture points as well.

Prior to showing up to class, make sure you have completed the assigned materials. If nothing has been assigned, read the relevant chapter in the course text. Most text chapters start with learning objectives. Make sure you understand each learning objective prior to class. This prework will make taking notes much easier. Plus, it will make it easier for you to connect the dots between the class lecture and the textbook objectives.

Keep your opinion out of it when taking class notes. Write down the professor's words and ideas, not yours. You might feel the urge to inject your ideas, thoughts, or concept while taking notes; don't do that. You will have plenty of time, later on, to put your personal touch on your notes.

Concentration and Focus Takes Effort

You are not going to be used to paying attention in a class for 50 minutes at a time or more. Some studies show that a student's attention span is actually only seven or eight seconds long, so you are going to find yourself drifting in and out. This is ok, just catch yourself and reengage in the lecture.

Some professors will try to dish out their information into blocks of time of fifteen-to-twenty-minute intervals, breaking things up with questions, surveys, or some other class activities. Unfortunately, in many classes, you will experience a constant stream of words coming at you. And here is another benefit of notetaking, the very activity of focusing on your notetaking will help you stay focused. Don't get distracted by other student's lack of focus, poor habits, or distracting behavior.

Your Class Lecture Follows a Storyline

Like a movie, your class lectures will follow a storyline. The first few minutes of the lecture and the last few minutes of the lecture are often the most important parts of the lecture. Your professor will generally tell you what they are about to tell you. Next, they will tell you what they want you to know. And then, in the end, they will summarize the lecture key points and tell you what they will cover in the next class.

Each lecture is just like its own story, with the main theme and subsequent supporting points. During the lecture, pay attention to the emphasis. Professors will often repeat important concepts, concepts they know will be on their tests and exams. They may use keywords or phrases, such as, "This is an interesting point," or "this is an important concept or idea," or "The key point for you to remember here is," or "You should keep this in mind" when you hear phrases like this, you want to make sure to write down these words just as the professor says them.

Don't Rely on Anybody Else's Notes

"But professor Stemmle, my professor, provides us with the class notes directly, or our bookstore sells us notes, or my sorority sister made an "A" in the class, and I have her notes, so I don't need to take my own notes."

Taking your own notes is the best way to not only pay attention in class, but it is the best way to engage and remember the key points of the lecture. Use other sources as a secondary source of information and a way to fill in any gaps you may have in your notes. Now, we want to tie all your notes together, so when it comes time to study, we have a clear and concise representation of what you will need to know.

46

Let's take a look at a simple way to do just that. On the left-hand side of your paper, you list the key concept or learning objective. In the next column, you will list the supporting information or points. And then finally, I want you to summarize the key ideas.

This simple system will help you reinforce your lectures and make studying for your tests or exams a breeze!

Engage in Class

Many of the larger universities are not set up for active student participation. They have large lecture halls with hundreds of students, and they may not only discourage questions but forbid them. In these institutions, you will have to email your questions to your professors, small group leaders, or teaching associates.

However, at most universities and colleges, the professors want your engagement, they want a free flow of ideas, they want to hear your opinions, thoughts, and ideas. If you have a question, ask it! If you think you can add something to the dialog, bring it up.

Look, the majority of professors don't want to lecture to blank stares. They are passionate about their topics, and they really enjoy an active dialog with students. Sometimes your class participation will actually be required.

Your syllabus will let you know if your professor requires your participation. In many of your college classes, your class participation will actually be required. Often participation requirements at the undergraduate level will range from 5%, 10%, or even 25% of your grade. In graduate school, it is not unusual for 50% of your grade to come from participation. If your professor throws out questions to the class, they are asking for your engagement. So, make sure you participate! Participation shows you care, shows you respect the professor, shows you value your time in class, and are valuing the professor's efforts.

47

Organize Your Life, Not Just Your Assignments

College has a way of shaking up your schedule, impacting your exercise, diet, sleep, and your study habits. You will be busy with your classes, clubs, friends, maybe even a job, and a seemingly endless number of other commitments. As such, it's can become very easy for you to become disorganized and overwhelmed!

The mistake that I see most college students make, though, is not organizing both their classwork, social life, and job in one simple and easy to use planner.

And as a result, it is not long before students start to miss their assignments and commitments they have. This quickly leads to stress and a feeling of being overwhelmed! You start to feel like you can't possibly get all you need to get done in the time that you have. Don't let this happen to you; you need to make your organization skills a priority!

View Every Class as Networking Opportunity

Your professor can help you not just become successful in the classroom, but they can help you find internships, write letters of recommendation on your behalf, and even help you network for your career. You should view your professor as someone you want to get on your team! A big part of college should be devoted to building your professional network, and what better way to start on that journey than by getting your professors in your corner!

I am amazed at the number of students who don't take their classes seriously. Later when they find out their professor has a relationship that can help them out, they are shocked when the professor will not write a letter of recommendation or pick up the phone to make an introduction. You must understand that professors have hundreds of students each semester; they have a limited number of favors they can call in from their network. They are only going to call in those favors for the best-performing students.

With that said, building a relationship with your professor will help you in many potential ways. Professors will be more likely to grant you an extension, provide you with feedback on an upcoming assignment, or help you with that test you bombed! It really is surprising just how few students try to build relationships with the faculty at their university. For the most part, students wait until they have an issue before seeking out the help of their professor. If you have an issue, you don't just want to be a number in a grade book. Build a relationship with as many professors as possible, as early as possible.

Contrary to popular belief, the vast majority of professors put in a lot of work to make your class experience a good one. They want to make an impact on their student's life, they are passionate about what they teach, and they are excited to be around other people who are passionate about their field. So, let's look at a few ways you can start to build relationships with your professors.

Say hello! I know this seems simple, but very few students will say hello to the professor as they walk into the room or lecture hall. An actual hello and smile can go a long way to start building a relationship.

If you missed them walking in the room, catch them before they leave, point out something you found interesting in the lecture, and make a connection. For instance, I really enjoyed the part about negotiating in today's lecture! I want to be a sports agent and learning to negotiate effectively will be critical to my success. I was wondering if you could you recommend a book or resource that I could dig deeper into to further develop my negotiating skills?

Show Interest in the Class

Sit in the front of the class, take notes, make eye contact, nod your head up and down when the professor makes an interesting point. You want to demonstrate you are engaged and interested in the class!

Ask a Question

Professors routinely pause during their lectures to give student's an opportunity to ask questions. This, not the time to ask, "Will this or that be on the test? Don't ask a question that they just spent the last 10 minutes talking about, and don't ask when your assignment is due when it is already in the syllabus. You want to ask a probing question, a question that shows you have reflected on the class lecture. Maybe you say something like, in the textbook, it said XYZ, about ABC. In your experience, do you find this is something that occurs frequently, or is it more of an outlier? The key here is you want to demonstrate to the professor that you did some prep work prior to coming to class, and you are interested in learning.

If You Are Asked a Question, Take a Shot at the Answer

Professors want engagement; they want to create a class dialog. They will throw out questions they hope will spur a useful class dialog. Often, the professor wants you to have a wrong or partially correct answer. They may want to demonstrate there is more than one answer. They might just want to demonstrate to the class just how difficult or misunderstood the topic really is. So, jump in and play along with an answer.

Volunteer

Professors almost always start student presentations by asking for volunteers, and they are almost always more generous in their grading to those students who go first, the ones who don't get the opportunity to learn and adapt from the numerous students that went before them.

Don't Limit Your Conversation to the Classroom

Does your professor show up early, hoping to connect with students? Do they hang out after class and chat with students? Do they encourage you to come by during their office hours? Do you pass them in the hall every MWF at 1:00 p.m.? Engaging in dialogs outside the classroom provides you extra time to connect and build relationships with your professors.

Offer to Help With Their Latest Project

Professors have limited resources to assist them with their tasks, research, and projects. Let your professors know you are passionate about their field of study and would love the opportunity to gain some practical experience by assisting them with what they are working on. Working on your professor's team is one of the best ways to build a relationship.

Don't Have Time to Help Out

It will not take long for your professor to bring up their research, book project, or social cause they are working on. Show an interest in their work. Professors, like most other people, love talking about the things they are passionate about.

Tell the Professor How Much You Enjoy Their Class

Make sure you are sincere, and you can point to something specific that you enjoyed about their lecture. For instance, I really enjoy your stories from your work experience. They really connect the class material for me and help me understand how I will be able to apply the material in my career.   If you are not really jazzed about the topic, you can tell them how you enjoy their passion and how that shines through in the lecture and makes the class engaging.

Participate in Your Major

Each department will have groups, activities, gatherings, lectures, or what have you throughout the semester. Show up and participate. If you're a marketing major, join the American Marketing Association group on campus. If you love marine science, attend the faculty lectures that are given as part of special events on campus.   Faculty members are required to do extra things as part of their service to the university, and they greatly appreciate and make a special mental note of students who engage in these activities; they even will often offer up extra credit to encourage students to attend.

Say Thank You

Thank your professor for their time, for responding quickly to your email, or if they helped you out in some way. Everybody likes to be appreciated, your professors included.

Stay on Top of New Happenings

Did some breaking news related to one of your class lectures occur?   Forward the article to your professor. Not only does this demonstrate your engagement, but it also provides your professor with some real-time info to work into their class lectures.

Become a Fan

You can read their books and published articles. Make mention of any awards or recognitions they have received. Professors like to have their accomplishments recognized. So, find a way to naturally bring up their work in a conversation. It can be as simple as saying, congratulations on receiving the XYZ grant or the ABC award. Maybe, you let them know how much you enjoyed reading their book or published article. Just find a simple way to recognize their work.

I am not suggesting you become a stalker! Just pick a few of these ideas that work for you and make building relationships with your professors a priority! Things will happen during the semester that will set you back and having solid relationships with your professors will be important when they do. One way to make sure you are always on top of things is to work hard to stay a class or two ahead. This way, if you get sick, get a massive headache, have to attend a funeral, or what have you, you won't fall behind. And if something serious does happen, you will have a chance to recover without ruining the whole semester.

You can ensure you stay organized by using your planner to know exactly when your assignments are due and then pulling assignments ahead with your own milestones to ensure you stay ahead in your classes. Getting ahead on your assignments will not only keep you less stressed but will also allow you to get more out of the class lectures and give you more time to make deeper connections among topics and ideas.

Concepts in college often build on each other, so preparing in advance allows you to be more prepared, allows you to make more valuable contributions in class, and help you be prepared for the unexpected.

If you are unorganized, you will become overwhelmed. If you get overwhelmed, you will become stressed. If you are stressed for too long, anxiety will kick in and jeopardize your well-being and college career.

However, you can prevent this negative cycle from getting out of control by organizing your time and efforts. Being organized allows you to do things in a timely manner. If you exercise self-discipline, you will eliminate the negative stress that comes from procrastination.

Attending class is vital to staying organized and achieving success in college. Attending class will allow you to stay prepared and to keep you from falling behind. Attending class will pay for itself many times over. If you must miss class, be aware of the attendance policies, and email your professor before you miss class if your professor does take attendance.

If you miss class, don't email your professor asking if you missed anything important. Professors find that question very insulting; if it wasn't important, they would not be spending their time on it in class.

Instead, talk to your classmates about what information you missed in class, borrow two or three students' notes because not everybody will be as diligent in their note-taking, and the different perspectives will help you narrow in on what information you need to focus on.

Make sure you catch up on your work before the next class. If you feel like you may be missing something or if you need clarification on your classmate's notes, go by your professor's office during office hours and ask for clarification.

Following these guidelines will have you well on your way to navigating your classes like a seasoned upperclassman.

Study Skills

Albert Einstein said this: "Never regard study as a duty, but as the enviable opportunity to learn."

Your education will give you knowledge of the world around you. It will help you develop a new way of looking at your life. It will help you develop intelligent opinions and points of view on important things in life.

The typical high school student's study habits are not only insufficient in college, but they are also downright counter-productive to your overall success in college. Learning outside the classroom accounts for the majority of your college education, yet most universities give little effort to teach you how to study or form proper strategies to achieve success.

We don't give much thought to the idea of studying as a process itself, a skill we need to develop. We usually apply the same old tools we used in high school, and we just think we can apply a little more effort in college to be successful. This is where metacognition is important to understand.

Metacognition is the complete process of thinking about your thinking and learning about your learning. Its focus is on identifying your learning goals, monitoring your progress, and getting help when you're confused, building momentum, and reviewing your results.

Metacognition is all about knowing yourself as a learner and using this awareness intentionally to learn at your best. Regardless of your learning style, study systems, and approaches, there are some foundational approaches that will work for you to improve your study results and the overall quality of your learning experience.

First, we need to start with the topic at hand; you want to identify the big ideas. To figure out the big ideas, ask yourself this question:

What is being said about the person, thing, or idea (the topic)? Next, identify the supporting ideas. And finally, you identify the supporting details.

Let's look at the following paragraph and try to identify the topic and the main idea.

Most college students are unsure about what they want to do for a career. It is a big decision. There are a number of things students can do to help identify their choices. For example, you can take an interest test, do some research on a potential career, do volunteer work in an area in which you are interested, or "job-shadow," in which you spend time with someone who is working in a field that interests you. These are just a few valuable ideas as you begin to choose a career. Picking a major goes a long way to helping you figure out what you want to do for a career. Research shows that students who seriously engage in the process of identifying a career during their first two years of college are 76.3% more satisfied with their chosen major and subsequent career choices.

In the above paragraph:

- The topic is career or job options.
- The main idea is the number of things to help the reader choose a career.
- The supporting idea is picking a major.
- The supporting details are research shows.

Universities and your professors want you to succeed, and as such, they put a lot of resources into creating tutoring and support centers for you. These resources are free and are typically staffed with high GPA students in your major or field of study. These students have had the course you are taking, heck they may have had the same professor, and these tutors can give you valuable insights into just what you can expect in the class and how you can best prepare.

Your professor or TA can review key concepts with you and go over the issues you had on the test, but they will not be able to be your tutor. I want you to head to the tutoring center often, use the center as a way to prevent problems, not recover from the problem.

Struggling to grasp a particular concept? Having difficulty working on a certain type of problem? Struggling to connect the dots between ideas? Head to the tutoring center at the first sign of any uncertainty or difficulty. You want to fix any of your potential areas of weakness or confusion before exam day, not after!

Successful students use tutors as partners in preparation, not partners in recovery. Tutors will help you recover, they will help you get back on course, but that is a much more difficult and stressful road to go down.

Make tutors partners in preparation, and you will not need to deal with the stress, pressure, and frustration of trying to recover from a bad grade. Universities know what classes students routinely struggle with and offer tutoring in those courses.

Go by and meet the tutors in the first couple of weeks of the semester. Ask the tutors where students typically struggle. Ask what concepts the teachers typically test that may be difficult. Ask for ideas on preparing for the course. Make visiting the tutoring center a part of your preparation process long before you ever need help.

Remember what mom said, "An ounce of prevention is worth a pound of cure," When it comes to using tutors, nothing could ring truer! Tutors have lots of valuable insights. Make sure you use this insight information to your advantage.

Studying requires your full attention and focus. If you are distracted by your roommates, crowds in your local Starbucks or even your own social media feeds, you will not be getting the most out of your studying time.   When you are studying, you need to be focused on your studies, not on what is going on around you.

Find a quiet spot to study, like the library on campus, or a study room on campus. You want to find anywhere where you can focus on your tasks with little distractions. Put your phone away while you study.   Interruptions don't just take up your time; they also degrade the overall quality of your efforts.

In two recent studies, college students were asked to write three essays based on prompts that were created by the College Board. Each participant was given 12 minutes to plan and outline their essays on paper, and they were given 12 minutes to write their essays using a computer.

While the students were working on their essays, the students were interrupted at random intervals with unrelated tasks and asked to solve things like math problems or to unscramble word riddles. Students were told to finish as much of the task as possible during each of the 60-second interruptions before they went back to working on their essays.

Each of these interruptions occurred during two of the three essays so that each of the participants completed an essay under each of the three test situations (i.e., no interruptions, interruptions during the planning phase, and interruptions during the writing phase).

The essays were then assessed by two trained graders based on a 0-6 scale drawn from the College Board Essay Scoring Guide. The researchers also analyzed the total number of words written and participants' accuracy on the interruption tasks.

In both of the interruption conditions, the essays received significantly lower ratings compared with the control condition. On average, the interrupted students received scores that were about half a point lower on the rating scale.

Another study found that when professors allowed phones or laptops in the lecture hall, final exam grades dropped by as much as 5 percent on average, or half a grade. This result held true even for those students who didn't actually use a device. When doing your schoolwork, do your schoolwork without distractions; your GPA and future self will thank you.

One of the more difficult things to figure out in college with your work is actually knowing when you are done. When you're eating a meal, you know when you are full. But when it comes to academic work, how do you know when you're done?

How do you know when you've finished reading an assignment? Sure, you got to the end, but what did you really absorb the material? How do you know when your paper is ready to turn in? How do you know when you've finished studying for an exam?

Well, here are some answers I have received from students:

- I just do.
- I trust in God.
- I've run out of time.
- When I can teach my roommate what I have learned.
- When I've highlighted, recopied my notes, ticked off all my flashcards, answered sample questions, and tested myself.

Now the last answer demonstrates the student has a system in place to be successful. And when you finish this book, you will have a system in place as well.

Each assignment will come with a rubric. The rubric outlines the requirements of the assignment and how your professor will grade the assignment. It is critical that you take the time to ensure you clearly understand your assignment's rubric. Understanding specifically what your professor is looking for is critical to creating an overall success plan regardless of your learning style.

For instance, with a reading assignment, you want to be clear on what you are supposed to do. Are you supposed to analyze the reading, summarize it, or do both? When you leave class, make sure you're clear on what's been assigned. You can actually waste a lot of time trying to figure out what the assignment is all about.

With a clear understanding of the assignment requirements, I like to use a trick I call the "time traveler" to understand just how much time and effort the assignment will require. I call it this because we will look at the past, present, and future to determine our knowledge gaps and effort.

The Past: Ask yourself what you already know. The Present: Ask yourself what you will need to learn. The Future: Ask yourself how you will approach learning the needed material and the time that will be required.

The less foundational knowledge we each have, the more we will need to learn, the more effort and preparation we will need to make to be successful. Learning to estimate the time required to tackle your individual assignments is a skill you want to develop. Before starting on an assignment, estimate the amount of time you believe it will take to complete that assignment, and compare that to the actual time you took to complete the assignment. Making this approach into this habit will allow you to develop better schedules and improve your time management skills.

Regardless of how well you prepare, there will be challenges. An effective way to work through confusing topics is to talk through your challenging material with yourself. Ok, I know the difference between A and B, but how does C work. Keep talking through things out loud and watch things clear up. Research supports that talking to yourself while studying is a very beneficial practice.

Great students are sticklers. Sticklers pay attention to details, they exceed the minimum requirements for their assignment, they want to make sure they have given their best effort.

You Need To Take Breaks

Taking structured breaks is critical to your success in college. The human attention span is limited. Humans now have shorter attention spans than goldfish. The goldfish is thought to have an attention span of nine seconds compared to eight for the average human student.

The chapter on time management will teach you some techniques to maximize your breaks and get the most out of your study sessions. But for now, just realize that it is important to structure your study and break time to achieve peak performance.

When studying, put a little variety into your study sessions by switching from one subject to another. Switch from one mode of studying to another to break things up. Go from writing to reading to self-quizzing, etc. Even switching locations from time to time can stimulate your brain to reboot.

Your approach to studying is important, but it turns out that when you study also has an impact on your GPA, and it is not just all-nighters that hurt your GPA. Research shows that each hour used for study during the day is equal to one and a half hours at night. Students who study between 6:00 p.m. and midnight are twice as likely to earn an "A" as students who put off studying until after midnight. Do you want to get the most out of your study time? Study earlier in the day!

Treat College Like a Job

Since most of you will be taking 12-15 hours a semester, and you will spend 2-3 hours outside of class for each hour in class, you will have a 24 to 45-hour a week job.

Create your schedule based on these expectations; don't try to back your schedule into the hours you have available on any day or week. Your education is your priority; schedule it as such!

Once you start studying, make a commitment to be fully focused, fully engaged, not just physically present. We already spoke about the importance of focus and lack of distractions. You must also raise your level of expectation. Give it all you have! Your future self will thank you!

We are all human, and despite your best efforts, there are times when you will have your back against the wall, where you will have too little time and too much work. When you find yourself in those circumstances, here is what you do.

The First step is what is called triage. Triage is making decisions about priorities. You have to determine the most important material, moderately important material, and least important material. What is the weight of the assignments you need to get done? An assignment worth 20% of your grade takes priority over an assignment that is 1% of your grade. Which classes will be impacted the most by a poor grade?

The key here is to identify those items which will have the most impact on your GPA. Now that you know what is important, you need to figure out what you don't know and prioritize your knowledge gaps, the things you don't know. The last step is to develop a study plan to fill in your gaps based on the time you have.

When you are short on time, it is critical you use all the time you have. Take your study notes with you everywhere you go, the shuttle, meals, breaks between classes, etc. Even small amounts of time will make a difference. The key here is to make the best use of all the time you do have available.

When you are short on time, you need to engage all your senses as much as possible. I call this taking a 360-degree approach. This strategy will allow you to get the most out of the time you do have. Taking a 360-degree approach means making every effort to listen, speak, read, and write the material, engaging all your senses.

Test Taking Skills

Test-taking is an integral part of your college experience, and your preparation will significantly determine how well you do. Prepare properly, and you will know you have that "A" locked up before you even walk into the exam room!

Preparation not only prepares you for the material, but it also goes a long way to reducing unhealthy test anxiety that many students face. If you are properly prepared, your stress levels will elevate, but only to a healthy level; your attention and focus will be enhanced. If you are not properly prepared, the stress you feel will surpass healthy levels, and this stress will negatively impact your performance.

This relationship between stress and performance is highlighted by The Yerkes–Dodson law. The law shows the empirical relationship between arousal and performance. The law dictates that performance increases with physiological or mental arousal, but only up to a point. When you pass that point, your performance starts to decline.

The key take away is to realize that stress is natural and healthy when maintained at an appropriate level. This is why it is so important to focus on preparation and maintaining a success mindset.

Preparation starts with each class syllabus. Too many students don't even read their syllabus. They may glance at it, plan to come back and read it, they may even print it and place it in their class folder, but few use it to organize and plan their semester. This is a huge mistake! The syllabus leaves all kinds of clues to ensure your success in the class. Your class syllabus will outline your course objectives, learning outcomes, class goals, and other important information. This information should serve as a roadmap for your preparation and will help you stay focused on what your professor believes is important. Let's look at a typical course objectives statement from a syllabus.

Course Objectives: The chief objective of marketing is to develop the student's understanding of the marketing function in for-profit, not-for-profit, and public sector organizations. Specific attention will be given to the following course objectives:

- Defining the components of the marketing function.
- Evaluating the marketing environment.
- Devising marketing strategy.
- Implementing marketing decisions in a complex and global marketplace.

If it is in the course objectives, rest assured you will be tested on it! You want to pull the course objectives from your syllabus and write them into your class notebook. During class lectures, you want to tie the key points of the lecture back to a course objective.

Next on the syllabus clue map are your student learning outcomes or SLOs. You can be sure that these concepts will all be tested as well. You want to map your SLOs to the applicable chapters in your class textbook. Make sure to align your SLOs with your class lecture notes and class assignments as well.

Many classes will have a project or an experiential learning component. The goal of these type of assignments will be outlined in your course syllabus as well. Usually, your professor will lecture on the syllabus concepts in class, and you will want to make sure you can tie your lectures back to these objectives as well.

The textbook providers provide all kinds of aids and resources for their professors. These resources are designed to highlight, explain, and test your course materials effectively. These resources often include providing presentations, tests, and quiz questions, along with other resources for student success. The provided resources and questions are designed to test student learning around each of the textbook's individual chapter learning objectives. Make sure you connect the dots between your class lectures, text assignments, and the textbook learning objectives.

Students often believe they just need to review their class notes from the professor's lectures, but they are shocked when they are tested on things not covered in the lectures. You are typically expected to put in two to three hours of work for every hour in class. Using your syllabus provides your roadmap of how to effectively invest that time.

With that said, professors will generally test what they talk about in class. They want to reward students for coming to class, and they like to make sure they are adding value beyond what is in the class text. Professors like to throw out questions in class that will show up on the test or exam. They like to see who is paying attention and engaged in the class lecture. Pay special attention to the questions the professors ask during the class lecture.

Many professors have teaching assistants (TA). These assistants often prepare and grade the class exams. Get to know your professor's TA's. TA's like to demonstrate how smart they are. TA's often will overshare and give you critical insights into what you will be tested on throughout the semester.

Professors often drop hints with their words. During the class lecture, they may say things like, this is interesting, an important fact is, let me repeat that, you might see this again, or what have you.

Make a special note of the ideas or concepts that follow or precede statements like these.

It is no state secret that many professors are lazy and often will reuse their prior test material. Ask around campus; many clubs and organizations maintain test banks. Even if the professors do change their questions often, reviewing prior tests gives you valuable insight into where that professor is diving deep and areas that are being given little emphasis.

But what if I do all that and I am just not good at taking tests? Most students who claim to be bad test takers are just bad preparers. They lack a system! They are haphazard in their approaches and are leaving too much learning to the last minute; they are not studying; they are starting to learn.

A proper system turns test prep into a review; without a system, students are stuck in learn mode, not prep mode. Let's look at 12 steps you can take to ensure you are successful with any test or exam.

Step 1

First, read the applicable chapter or assignments prior to the class lecture. By reviewing the class material prior to the lecture, you enter the lecture with a solid foundational understanding of the topic. You understand what you understand. You know exactly where you are confused. And when the professor covers those topics, he or she will clear up the confusion for you, or you can ask clarifying questions to clear it up. This approach allows you to get the most out of your class time and greatly reduces the amount of time you actually have to invest outside the classroom, trying to play catch up.

Step 2

Work sample problems prior to the class lecture. Working sample problems is extremely important in your STEM classes. When you just read the concepts and ideas, you gain a general understanding, but what you need is a practical and functional understanding of the material. You need to be able to fully understand the concepts from multiple perspectives and scenarios. To achieve this level of understanding, you must work on problem sets. By working on the problem sets ahead of time, you know where your challenges are. You can ask intelligent questions in class and have your professor clarify things for you. You will be less likely to get lost in class and fall behind in the lecture. Remember, most concepts in STEM build on each other. Get lost in one lecture, and you likely will be lost in the next lecture, and so on.

Step 3

Third, some of your classes may not give you the opportunity to ask questions, so you will want to note any concepts, problems, or ideas you may be struggling with within your class notebook. If the professor doesn't clear these questions up during the lecture, you want to immediately head to the tutoring center or get with your professor or TA prior to the next lecture. Do not enter a new lecture with an unanswered question from a previous lecture.

Step 4

Fourth, take detailed notes during the lecture. Less is not more when it comes to note-taking. Note-taking not only helps you prepare for the class, but it also helps you stay focused and avoid distractions. As I previously mentioned, make sure you keep your opinions out of the mix here. You want to capture your professor's words, not yours.

Step 5

If the professor doesn't clear up any questions you have during the lecture, ask questions. Many times, students believe they understand something, and then they find out they didn't understand the topic as well as they thought they did. Make sure to take advantage of the opportunity to ask questions. You can be assured that if you have a question, other students do as well, so don't worry about being judged!

Step 6

Any time you are not able to follow an answer you receive in class, or while the professor was trying to clear things up, and you just found yourself more confused, you need to seek help. If this happens, go to the tutoring center and clear things up. If you are still struggling with the concepts after visiting the tutoring center, go see your TA or professor and walk them through your struggles and the actions you have taken to clear things up. Often your TA or professor can provide another point of view.

Step 7

But what if I do all that and I am still struggling? Well, go see your professor during their office hours. Explain the action you have taken and the work you have done, explain you are still struggling, and are hoping the professor can give you additional guidance in solving your problems. It is critical you show your professor you are working hard and just did not get frustrated after 3 minutes of effort and showed up in their office. 90% of professors' time is spent with the 10% of students who are putting in no effort. Show you are making an effort, and your professor will rally behind you.

Step 8

Turn your class notes into study cards. During the time you are working on your assignments, I want you to take your class notes and turn them into study cards. This approach will make preparing for your exams much more efficient and stress-free. By following this process, you ensure your study time will be actual study time, not preparation time.

Review your study cards as the semester progresses. The best way to prepare is like an athlete. An athlete is in a constant state of training. They don't wait until two days before the big game and go... ok, let's get started. So why would you wait until right before the exam for you to get started? By continually reviewing your note cards, you will be keeping the material front and center in your mind. Come test time, you are relaxed, you have learned your material, and you are in simple review mode. If you start to feel bad or have a personal issue pop up, you will not face a major setback; you are already prepared.

Step 10

Prior to the exam, attend the test review. Many professors or their TAs will conduct a test review prior to the exam. These reviews should not be skipped. These reviews often go over each question or topic on the exam. These reviews also give you the opportunity to learn about the test format, not just the material. The insights gained from these reviews are critical in properly preparing for an exam.

Step 11

Work sample test problems, or if none are provided, create your own. The internet is truly your friend here. With a quick google search, you can find sample questions on your exam topic, videos explaining the problems and solutions, and tips and tricks your professor may not have covered in class.

Step 12

Align your approach with the format of the test. The work required for multiple-choice versus short answer, problem sets, or essays is significantly different. There is a big difference in being required to recognize the right answer versus creating and supporting the correct answer. If your test will require you to write essays, practice writing likely essay questions. If your test will require you to support your work, practice properly supporting your work. The key here is to replicate the actual test as closely as possible in your preparation.

The Week Before Exams

With the 12-step system in place, let's look at how to handle the week leading up to your test or exam. Start studying a week before the exam, as this will give you time to break your material into manageable chunks you can easily digest. It takes time to develop a deep understanding of the material, which will make it much easier to recall. Make sure you get all your study materials prepared and organized ASAP.

You can't study right if you don't know what to study. Be sure to know what materials you will be tested on. Does this test include material from the last test, outside readings, videos, lectures, etc.? Know the weights of the topics on the test. What percentage of the exam is devoted to each type of question? The more information you can gather, the more effective you will be in your preparation. Identify your knowledge gaps and get to work in closing those gaps.

Get plenty of sleep the night before any test or exam, and make sure to eat and hydrate before your test. Your brain will work better with rest and a balance of carbs, protein, and water.

Bring a bottle of water for the exam; staying hydrated improves performance significantly. Studies show 8 to 10 cups of water a day improves brain performance by as much as 30 percent.

Quickly scan the whole exam before starting the test, so you have a feel for the overall test requirements and effort. Based on your review, you can budget your time to make sure you will have ample time to complete the work. You don't want to get stuck spending too much time on a question you can't seem to figure out and then run out of time and miss questions you knew the answer to but just never got the time to get to. If you have 60 minutes and 60 questions, you know you can't spend more than an average or one minute a question. Mark any questions you are struggling with, and come back to those.

Don't waste time if you don't know the answer; move on. If you are stuck mid-way through a problem, move on. Come back to the question with a fresh perspective after you have answered all the other questions. Often, something in another question will trigger an answer for a previous question you were stuck on.

For your multiple-choice questions, I want you to eliminate the obviously wrong answers, but I don't want you to guess an answer just yet. Go through the complete test before coming back to guess at the answers. Often, the answer to one question may be found in another question or answer list on the exam. You want to answer all the questions you know first, come back and guess at your multiple-choice questions, and then work any problem sets or essays you were stuck on

Make sure you answer the exact question asked. Many students will write all about the topic at hand in an effort to demonstrate all they know, but in their effort to provide a brain dump of information, they fail to answer the actual question asked. In high school, you might have gotten away with this. In college, this approach will not work. Answer the question asked clearly and concisely.

Take the time to make your points clear and easy to understand. Use titles, subtitles, and bullet points and avoid long run-on sentences and paragraphs. If your essay requires an introduction, hypothesis, three supporting points, and a conclusion, make sure these are all properly outlined in your essay. The key point here is not to make the professor or TA have to go on a scavenger hunt to grade your paper; it will cost you.

Bring in examples from class lectures, homework, readings, and activities into your answers, as this will show you were engaged and paying attention. Some creative efforts here will likely impress the professor.

Write your answers in clear and simple language. Don't try to show the professor how broad your vocabulary is or use big words like mayonnaise! Keep your language and writing clear and concise.

Remember to stay calm. Some questions are meant to challenge and even frustrate you, so take a deep breath and stay calm. Some professors may actually put a question on an exam they don't expect you to know the answer to, they may be trying to gauge your thought process, they might be trying out a few new questions to see if they are too difficult, and they may plan to exclude those from your test grade altogether. Often if the top students miss the same question, the professor will throw that question out altogether.

Don't be psyched out by those students that leave early or after only a few minutes. I see students get frustrated when they see other students finishing way ahead of them. Ignore it. Most of those students are throwing in the towel as they know they will receive a bad grade anyway.

Avoid the pretest chatter; "I don't understand this or that," "Is that going to be on the exam," "I studied for a week," "I didn't study at all," "I heard nobody can pass this test," and what have you. It is not productive and will just stress you out, so avoid it altogether.

Make it an easy, stress-free process to grade your paper. Low stress on the grader makes for higher grades.

- Provide a clear roadmap.
- Number the questions you are answering.
- Label sections you are answering.
- Divide your essay into clear paragraphs.

- Write as neatly as possible. A grader needs to be able to read your answers.

The key to acing exams is clearly in proper preparation, but regardless of your preparation, you still need to execute on test day. Employing these test-taking strategies, coupled with your hard work and discipline, will build your confidence and your GPA. Knowing you are prepared for the test reduces your stress and leads to you performing at your best.

Time Management Skills

Time Management does make all the difference in succeeding in college, graduating on schedule, enjoying this time in your life. Poor time management lead to students completely struggling and being stressed out. And maybe even like 50% of students who enter college, completely dropping out altogether.

Time Management in college is tricky; you have this illusion of time, but it is just an illusion. In college, it is not unusual for 40% to 50% of your grade to be earned in the last month of a semester. While you are cruising along with little care at the start of the semester, that last month is out there looming, waiting to reap havoc on your GPA.

This last month's effect is like a mountain that has accumulated snow over the winter months. A slight change in conditions can bring about an avalanche. What seemed like a manageable workload has now spun out of control. The avalanche is upon you.

Proper Time Management is all about breaking your assignments, tasks, and commitments for the entire semester into smaller chunks or milestones and smoothing out your required effort over a longer period of time. For instance, instead of waiting for the week before a paper is due, we break that paper into three smaller milestones and work on it over three weeks.

The key concept for you to recognize is that you need to manage the entire 16-week semester, not just the week that is in front of you. This is one of the biggest mistakes I see students make; their planning horizon is just way too short. They see what is in front of them for the current week, and then at some point in the semester, they realize they have three major assignments due in three different classes and a test in another class, the panic sets in, and the GPA decline starts, you don't want this to happen to you!

Life happens, you will get sick, a parent or grandparent will have a health issue, you may have to pull that extra shift at work, your buddy, the squirrel, might go missing. When the unexpected happens, you will have kept life manageable and within control by staying ahead in your classwork.

Despite my warnings to stay ahead of the game, you would be shocked to learn the number of times a student has come to me and said they couldn't turn in a project that they were supposed to be working on the entire semester because they had left their project to the very last week of the term and some life event happened.

Even if that life event had not occurred, they would be lucky to even pass the assignment given the hole they dug for themselves by waiting until the last minute. College can be stressful enough; don't let poor planning, procrastination, and lack of discipline derail your future.

Expanding your planning time horizon is so critical because, in college, your structure goes away. The learning pyramid is flipped upside down compared to high school. In college, you do about 20% of your learning in class and about 80% of your learning out of class. This very fact alone should tell you just how important planning your entire semester is to your overall success.

In college, too many students learn the hard way that they can't throw their assignments together at the last minute and expect to make a good grade or even a passing grade for that matter.

We all probably wish that there were more hours in a day, but since that is impossible, we must make the best use of the hours that we do have.

By utilizing a time management system, you will be well on your way to achieving better time management skills and becoming an all-around better college student.

You can start by organizing all your tasks, so you will know exactly what tasks to tackle and when they need to be worked on and completed. No student should tackle their course work without a daily planner.

Keeping a calendar is pretty straightforward, but surprisingly I have discovered most students don't keep one their first semester or two. If they do keep one, it is usually just a class schedule with locations, so they know when and where to go until they get their routine committed to memory. There is a big difference between having a planner and having a time management system!

The first thing I want you to do is to take your syllabi from each class and markdown (in pencil) all your assignments for the semester in your planner, don't forget mid-term and final exams.

Next, I want you to use different color highlighters for each of your classes (Math, English, Communications, etc.) and highlight your assignments in your planner. Don't use a green highlighter during this process; we will use a green highlighter later in our planning process.

Next, identify areas where you have multiple assignments, tests, exams, etc., all clustered together in a particular week or day. These clusters allow you to see right up front where you are going to be stressed and have little time.

If you are like most students, you will see a convergence around spring and fall breaks and the last month of the semester. Take a deep breath and don't panic!

Now we want to pay attention to the weights of our assignments. Review your syllabi for each class and underline in red in your planner all your significant assignments. Significance is subjective, and each class will vary, but anything that is 10% of your grade or higher should qualify.

Next, you need to enter your class schedule dates and times. Once we have our core class schedule logged, we have to estimate the time requirements for our study and assignments. Use two hours of study time for each hour of class time as your baseline requirement for scheduling your weekly class work.

Adjust this baseline target up or down based on your comfort and the difficulty of your class material. If you struggle with Math, you should bump up your baseline to three hours. If you are an English expert, you can adjust the baseline down to one hour or maybe 1.5 hours.

We now want to schedule your study time right into the planner. Planning a specific study schedule is key to avoiding procrastination. If you work or play sports and have that weekly commitment, schedule it now. Keep track of your study and assignment hours so that you can make adjustments throughout the semester.

Now we want to identify the areas on your calendar where you have little or no assignments due. Highlight these areas in Green in your Planner. These are the areas we are going to utilize to pull forward work you previously underlined in red and the areas where you have lots of things converging.

Look for those large significant assignments and break them down into smaller chunks with new due dates you create for yourself; these are called milestones. By utilizing your green areas, you will balance your workload, ensuring you reduce future stress and have the time available to do your best work.

Schedule fun just like you would do your work or assignments. If you know you are going to go out with your friends on Friday and Saturday nights, make sure you schedule that time. If you are going to be out too early morning hours and then sleep until 2:00 p.m., plan for that. Be realistic and don't set yourself up to fail by scheduling 4 hours of study time every Saturday morning when you already know you will be sleeping until early afternoon. The idea of planning is not to eliminate fun. It is to eliminate stress, anxiety and missed or poor-quality assignments by making sure you have a complete handle on all your responsibilities and activities.

Now that we have everything organized and scheduled, you now need to enter everything into your smartphone calendar and set up your alert notifications. These electronic alerts will keep you on schedule and ensure that you won't miss any of your assignments or milestones should you happen to forget to look at your calendar one day. Online notifications are your safety net to ensure you don't miss assignments. But our planner ensures we do proper planning and ensures we effectively utilize our time.

It is important to realize class syllabi are guidelines, and in many instances, the due dates and assignments will change. You will want to make sure you prepare for that new last-minute paper the professor decided to throw at you during the last month of classes. Yes, it happens more often than you will like.

It is important students get at least one day ahead in their classes as soon as possible. Things happen, schedules change, etc., but by building in a day buffer, you are preparing for that unplanned event that will inevitably occur at some point during the semester.

Pick a day each week to review the week and month ahead. Many students find Sundays work best for this review. Remember to schedule calendar review time and treat this time like you would any other required commitment. Use this time to clean up your email inbox and check and see if any of your professors have made schedule changes for the week ahead.

The critical activity in this weekly review is to establish the specific activities and work you will perform during your allotted calendar time slots. Initially, we just blocked off the time we knew we would need. Now that we have learned the specifics, we can schedule the activities and tasks we need to complete during the week.

As an example, we can take the 3 hours we have scheduled to study for a particular class and break down how we are going to use those three hours. Are we going to review our note cards, read a chapter in the text, work on a paper, or other tasks you have prioritized?

You just can't depend on your weekly reviews alone. Each day before noon, review your next day's schedule and check your school email account. If something new has popped up on your schedule that you forgot about something, etc., checking the next day's activities and your email early enough, you leave yourself time to course-correct if needed.

Many students mistakenly check their next day's calendar just before going to bed. If they have made a mistake or missed something, they have no time to correct their error, stress levels rise, they don't sleep well, and their next day's performance suffers. Students often don't get consistent emails sent to their university accounts, so they can get out of the habit of checking their school email and can miss valuable information. Don't let this deter you from sticking to the process. I recommend you set up alerts on your phone, so you know when you get an email to your university account.

Most students struggle with structure, and that is natural. By creating a schedule, you are not somehow magically sucking all the fun out of your life. In fact, you are reducing your stress and improving your performance, which will allow you to enjoy yourself a whole lot more.

You will miss study sessions and other events on your calendar; that is ok. It is very valuable to know you missed an event as opposed to the alternative of fooling yourself into thinking you are on track. If you miss something, plan to make it up. If you can't make it up, identify what caused you to veer off course. Make sure you learn and adjust things going forward.

Like any other skill, your organizational skills can be learned and improved. The most difficult part is breaking your lifelong bad habits. The key to getting better organized is to start with one small step and then take others one at a time.

You may find that what you've put off for days takes only takes a few minutes to complete. And once you see the benefits in one part of your life, you'll be motivated to expand this practice.

All the time management and organization tips in the world can only help if you put them to use. Procrastinating can be one of the biggest mistakes college students can make. Another common mistake is being unrealistic in their approaches.

The Eisenhower Matrix

When Dwight Eisenhower became the 34th president of America, he had already accumulated a great deal of knowledge on how to deal with difficult tasks and manage his time effectively. Dwight Eisenhower was a general in World War Two and became the supreme commander of the allied forces. Some would argue that he had the most important position of any general that ever served.

It became apparent to Eisenhower that he needed a system to do the most effective job that he could. In this regard, he came up with what is now known as the Eisenhower Matrix. This matrix has withstood the test of time and still one of the most effective tools to ensure you get things done.

The matrix is actually a four-quadrant box. You draw out a large rectangle, you then divide it into four parts.

THE EISENHOWER MATRIX

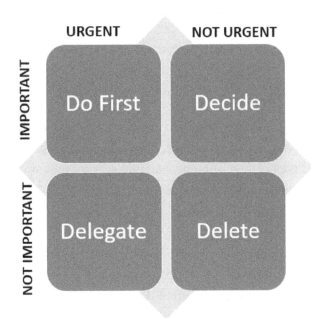

Part one in the upper left-hand corner is labeled, "Do First." Next to that, on the right side, you write, "Decide."

Under the "Do First" box, you write, "Delegate." The last box is the lower right- hand one, and in it, you write, "Delete."

Now we are going to write outside the box. This is where we label our priority. Quadrant one is the top priority, so over the top of that, we write, "Urgent." On the left-hand side of that Quadrant, we write, "Important."

Now we are going to label two more Quadrants. Over the top of Quadrant two, which says, "Decide," we will write, "Not Urgent." Now go to the Quadrant in the lower left-hand corner, which is labeled, "Delegate." On the outside of that Quadrant, write, "Not Important."

Quadrant One is your first priority. These tasks are of utmost importance in our personal lives, pursuing our degree, or whatever we may do to make a living.

Quadrant Two is where you do the actions that will make your goals and dreams come true.

Quadrant Three is where you delegate tasks to others. The tasks may have some importance, but they don't have the same weight as Quadrant two.

Quadrant Four is the Deleting Aspect. You have tasks in here that can be removed permanently or greatly reduced. Tasks in here are mostly entertainment tasks.

The Pomodoro Technique

Another tool at your disposal to manage your time is called the Pomodoro Technique, and this technique has become very popular in time management. In fact, it so popular that different versions of it are used to diffuse procrastination as well.

To get started, you need to be focused, so shut off your cellphone and close your browsers on any other device. You really want a quiet environment, so if you have noise distractions that cannot be turned off, consider wearing noise reduction headphones.

In using the Pomodoro technique, you start by deciding what the first important task of the day is. Then you set a timer for 20 minutes and focus 100% on that task.

When the timer chimes, set the timer for five minutes and check your phone or stretch out your body for five minutes. When this timer goes off, set the timer, and jump back in for another twenty minutes and then repeat the five-minute break. These 20-minute sprints are called Pomodoro's.

After doing four sets of twenty minutes, with your five-minute breaks in between, you are done. If you have more work to do, take a minimum of a 30-minute break and start the process over.

Learn to Say No

Another key to successfully managing your time is learning to say no. Many students have a hard time telling people no. Research shows that the harder you find it to say no, the more stress you incur. But here is the thing, the act of not saying no enough can invoke a triple threat to your health. It can lead to depression, stress, and even burnout. When your brain has to constantly search for ways to get around saying no to a request, it releases stress chemicals.

As a student, you are trying to build your resume and gain experience, so saying no can sound like a counterintuitive idea, but you need to realize that one of the keys to being productive and managing your time is to reduce the number of activities you are involved with that don't align with your current goals. Say no to the distractions, the things that don't move you closer to your goals.

If you want to dig deeper into the topic of time management, please read my best-selling book, *"Time Management Secrets for College Students."* Head over to Amazon and get a copy now!

Paper Writing Skills

You will write a lot of papers in college, and developing a system is key to ensuring you continually improve as a writer and make great grades. There are five steps to writing great papers in college, and these steps are:

1. Prewriting.
2. Your First Draft.
3. Revisions.
4. Editing and Proofreading.
5. Review for Submission.

Let me start by saying that each student writes differently. As a bestselling author, I get the opportunity to work with a lot of authors, and as a college professor, I see hundreds of papers every semester.

Some writers need to talk about their ideas, while others like to keep their ideas to themselves; still, others need to establish written outlines early on in the process, and others just like to do what I call a complete brain dump by writing pages of general ideas and concepts.

There really is no one better style, but there are proven processes you can follow to ensure your end product is high quality and meets the actual requirements of the assignment. As you continue to write papers in college, your own particular style and approach will emerge.

Each writing assignment you are giving will present its own special challenges. Some of the questions to consider are:

- Is the topic given to you, or can you pick your own?
- Are there a few topics you can choose from?
- Do you have experience or detailed knowledge of the topic?
- How difficult will the topic be to understand?
- Is there a lot of data easily available for your research?
- What format will your paper have to be written in?
- How complex is the rubric?
- How much time do you have?

The answers to these basic questions will provide a foundation for your approach to each individual assignment. Regardless of your approach, writing never follows a straight line. Writing is a forward as well as a backward activity, don't expect to move directly through the steps in the writing process.

Good writing will include rework, redevelopment, and sometimes a complete redo. Writing is like any other skill; it takes a lot of practice to become good at it. If you want to develop your skillset, you need to embrace the following four strategies.

- Read on a regular basis.
- Write each day.
- Pick topics that you are interested in.
- Be patient.

Prewriting Process

First, <u>Review the Rubric</u> – Understanding the paper requirements is key to writing a great paper. You need to ensure the topic you pick aligns well with the requirements for the assignment.

Next, <u>Pick a Meaningful Idea</u> – One that interests you, one that actually will add value to your education process.

<u>Learn as Much as You Can</u> – Once you've selected a subject, you need to research and gather information, ideas, and concepts to ensure you can meet the requirements of the rubric.

Next, <u>Determine Your Focus</u> – Express your focus in a thesis statement, a statement that helps you map out your paper.

Now you are ready to <u>Develop an Outline</u> – An outline provides an overall plan and helps you organize the flow of your paper. If your rubric provides an outline, follow it. If the rubric calls for particular section titles or subtitles, use those to the letter. Don't get creative here; follow any roadmap provided.

With your outline in hand, don't delay; you want to <u>Start Quick</u> - Write your first draft while your prewriting efforts are still front and center in your mind.

One very important thing to remember is that <u>First Impressions do Matter</u> - Put extra effort into your opening paragraphs. Professors will often read your opening and closing paragraphs closely and scan the body of your paper to ensure you followed the rubric. By putting extra effort and attention into your opening and closing paragraphs, you can greatly improve your grade.

<u>Always Reserve the Right to Get Smarter</u> – New ideas may develop as you write, don't be afraid to rework your outline or thesis.

Remember that Great is The Enemy of Good – Don't try to get everything right during your first draft; concentrate on developing your ideas.

Revising Your Paper

Review Your First Draft – Check your structure against the rubric, identify ideas that are not fully developed or supported with sources.

Go to The Writing Lab – On most college campuses, there is a writing lab. The writing lab is a critical resource. They will help you restructure your ideas, ensure your paper flows, and make further structural recommendations to improve your paper. In many cases, they will send an email to your professor, letting them know you came to the writing lab. Professors do take note of the students who go the extra mile to write a great paper.

Open and Close Review – Carefully review the quality of your opening and closing paragraphs. These paragraphs are the first and last impressions the grader will form, so make them good.

Upgrade Your Sources – Look for opportunities to improve the strength of your citations. Citations are important in supporting your work, so make sure they are strong and fully documented.

Get in the Flow – Edit your writing for smoothness and word choice. Does everything seem to flow and connect smoothly?

Check for Errors – Check for errors in usage, punctuation, capitalization, spelling, and grammar. Software like Grammarly is critical as a partner in your writing. Without it, you are at a competitive disadvantage.

Rubric Review – Look for the rubric requirements and look for any inconsistencies you may have in your paper.

<u>Final Review</u> – Now give your paper one last read, have another student review your paper, and offer to review theirs. Proofreading your own work is a difficult process.

<u>The Deadline is Not a Suggested Submission Time</u> – Make sure you submit your paper well ahead of the deadline. Papers submitted close to the deadline give the impression you procrastinated, were hurried, and waited to the last possible minute to write your paper.

<u>Decide if You Should Publish</u> - You will write a lot of papers in college; you should use those efforts for more than just a grade. Publishing your work on sites like LinkedIn can help establish you as a thought leader in your field, help grow your network, and set yourself up for internships or job success.

Let's look at some tips to help you make the most of your writing assignments.

Tip 1 - Accept That Good Writing Takes Time

Writing a good paper requires a significant amount of research, planning, writing, reflecting, and revising. In order for you to allow the process to unfold effectively, you need to plan and leave ample time to work through the process.

Tip 2 - Good Writing Requires Good Research

A lot of information is required to write great papers. The more you learn and know about your topic, the easier it is to write about it. Gather up as much information as you can during the prewriting stage.

Tip 3 - Good Writing is Focused

Limit the scope of your subject. It is exceedingly difficult to write an effective paper about a general subject like marketing. Where would you start? Where would you end? But if you limit the subject to a specific aspect or area of marketing, let's say, the use of affiliate marketing in the retail industry, you will find it easier to manage your paper.

Tip 4 - Good Writing is a Process of Learning & Discovery

Take some risks. Don't be afraid to pull in some personal experiences, stories, or connections you have with the subject or even take an extra step. For example, you could conduct a personal interview to provide a unique perspective or insight into your topic.

Tip 5 - Slow Down

The magic really happens as you start to develop a deeper understanding of your topic, and this takes time. When you are adding, deleting, rewriting, and restructuring your first draft, you are immersed in the process. This process takes time, and quality rarely emerges on your first pass.

Let's Look at the Traits of Effective Writing

Effective writing presents interesting information about the subject. It has a clear purpose and focus; it has an overall vision for what is being said. The ideas are well developed and hold the reader's attention.

Good writing has a logical organization. It has a clearly developed beginning, middle, and end. Each point is supported with examples, details, explanations, and definitions.

Good writing is unified. The overall structure of the ideas unifies the paper and makes the writer's objectives crystal clear.

In strong writing, you can hear the writer's voice, their unique way of expressing ideas, concepts, and emotions. It creates a specific and unique personality or imprint.

With good writing, nouns and verbs are specific. The modifiers are limited but colorful. The overall language helps communicate the appropriate tone for the work. Good writing flows from sentence to sentence. But it is not predictable. Sentences vary in length and they don't all start the same way.

Sentence variations give a rhythm to your writing, and that makes your paper more enjoyable to read, creating a happy professor, and of course, a better grade!

Good writing follows the rubric. Is APA formatting required, or maybe AMA or MLA formatting is required? What is the required length? What is the number of sources required? What is the type of required sources? What font is required?

Good writing meets the standards for punctuation, mechanics, usage, and spelling. Good writing is well-edited to ensure the work is accurate and easy to follow.

Even If your writing is great, but it fails to meet the standards outlined in the rubric, your grade will greatly suffer. In fact, some professors may give you a zero and not even bother to read your paper if you have not properly formatted your paper or used the correct number of citations, etc.

How to Select a Topic

Selecting a topic for your paper is very important for your overall success. The following strategies will help you select a specific topic for your paper that will set you up for success from the beginning.

Understand the Paper's Purpose – Are you writing to describe, persuade, explain, entertain, or retell?

Do a quick Self-evaluation – How do you feel about the subject? Do you have enough interest and time to address the subject thoroughly?

When it Comes to Your Paper's Subject – How much do you already know about the topic? Can you think of an interesting way to write about the topic? Is there a lot of information readily available on your topic?

Think About Your Audience – Who are your readers? A Professor, TA, scholarship committee? How much do they already know about the subject? How can you get them interested quickly?

Think About Form and Style – How will you present your ideas? A narrative, a report, or an essay? Can you develop an interesting hook?

Journaling is a Powerful Tool to Capture Ideas – Writing your thoughts, feeling, and ideas in a journal on a daily basis is a great way to capture potential ideas for papers. Underline ideas in a journal that you would like to explore further. Paying attention to things that spark an emotion in you can be a great source of ideas for future papers.

Freewriting – Freewriting is another powerful tool to uncover topics to write about. Write down your thoughts for 5 to 10 minutes to discover possible writing ideas. Begin by writing thoughts that are related to the class or assignment specifics. Don't stop to judge, edit, or make any corrections. If you get stuck, write, "I am stuck" and start thinking about another subject and start throwing out ideas there. Whatever pops in your head, write it down. At the end of your time, underline any ideas that have merit to explore further.

Brainstorming – You can also begin with a single thought or keyword related to your assignment and simply start listing ideas. Get a group together have everyone start throwing out ideas and topics.

Begin by listing and brainstorming a cluster of words with a nucleus word related to your topic. Then cluster ideas around the nucleus word. Circle or highlight each idea you write and draw a line connecting it to the closest related idea. After three or four minutes, look for ideas to explore in free writing.

Emotion Can Drive Good Ideas

<u>Write About What Makes You Angry</u>

- Core curriculum got you down? Write about it.
- Parking a big issue on campus? Write about it.
- Cost of education putting you in debt? Write about it.
- Upset that the drinking age is 21? Write about it.
- Bothered that you must live on campus your freshman year? Write about it.
- Upset student-athletes can't be paid? Write about it.
- If it makes you angry, you are less likely to procrastinate, take short cuts, and be bored.

<u>Write About What You Care About</u>

- Are you passionate about gender equality?
- Term limits?
- Education?
- Entrepreneurship?
- Religion?
- Travel?
- Fashion?
- Entertainment?

If you care about the issue, you will be more engaged, less likely to procrastinate, take short cuts, and be bored during the process.

Before getting started, you want to gather your thoughts. Here are a few ways to get started.

Argue For or Against Your Idea – What do you like about it? Not Like about it? What are the strengths and weaknesses?

Describe it - What do you see, feel, hear, taste, smell?

Compare it – What is it similar to? What is it different from?

Analyze it – What are the trends, the history, beliefs, social impact, economic impact?

Associate it – What connections can you make?

Apply it – What can you do with it? How can you use it?

Utilize Some Popular Tools

- Visual organizers are another tool that can be very helpful to help you gather and organize your thoughts for writing.
- Clustering or mind maps are also extremely effective visual organizers as well.
- The Cause/Effect Diagram is used to collect and organize details for a cause/effect thesis.
- The Timeline is used to collect details for personal narratives and for papers recalling important events.
- The Fishbone Diagram is used to map out problem solution assignments.
- The Venn Diagram is used to collect details to compare two subjects.
- The Process or Cycle Diagram is used to collect details for science or operational related writing, usually applied to describe how a process or cycle works.

- The Sensory Chart is used to collect details for descriptive and observation assignments.
- The Definition Diagram is often used to gather information for extended problem sets.
- The Line Diagram is used to collect and organize details.

Forming Your Thesis Statement

A thesis statement simply identifies the focus of your writing. We can look at a simple formula for drafting a successful thesis statement. A specific subject, plus a specific condition, stand, or feeling, equals an effective thesis statement.

If you try to cover too much ground in your writing, it may be too difficult to follow. This is why it is so important to establish a well-focused thesis for your writing assignments. For illustrative purposes, let's say your assignment is a paper about opportunities available to college students.

An example of a specific subject would be college internships.

Your thesis statement here would be: College internship programs (specific subject) benefits students in three ways (specific features).

With a clear thesis in place, you next need to develop a writing plan before you start work on your first draft.

The first thing you want to evaluate is your thesis statement. Often, your statement will point you in a logical direction.

Next, review your support for your thesis. See if an overall plan of attack begins to emerge.

Finally, consider the eight-core methods of organization.

1. Chronological order (time) is an effective approach for sharing personal narratives, explaining events, or summarizing steps.
2. Order of location (spatial) is useful for descriptions. Details can be described from right to left, from top to bottom, from the center to the edge, etc.
3. Illustration (deductive) you first state your thesis or general idea and follow with facts, reason, and examples.
4. Climax (inductive) is an approach where you present specific details, followed by a general statement or conclusion.
5. Compare/Contrast is an approach in which you compare one subject to another subject. You highlight how the subjects are alike and how they are different.
6. Cause/Effect is a type of arrangement that helps you make connections between a result and the events that came before it. Typically, you begin with a general statement giving the cause of something, and then you discuss specific effects.
7. Problem/Solution is a type of organization in which you state a problem and explore possible solutions
8. Classification or Definition is an organization method that can be used to explain a concept or term. Start by placing your subject in the right class, and then you will provide details that show how your subject is different from and similar to others in the same class.

Your First Draft

Write as much of your first draft as possible in one session while all of your preparation work is still fresh in your mind. Concentrate on developing your ideas, not producing a final copy. Make sure to include as much detail as possible. Continue writing until you make all your main points, or you reach a logical stopping point.

Your first draft shows you how well you align with your rubric and sets the ball in motion for the development of an "A" paper.

As a Starting Point: You are ready to write your first draft when:

- You are well versed in your topic.
- When you have established your thesis.
- And you have organized your supporting ideas.

Ideas – Develop all the relevant thoughts and ideas you have or alternative directions you may have. Remember, a first draft is your first look at developing your writing ideas, so be flexible with your thoughts and approaches.

Organization – Use your prewriting and planning as a general guide when you write. Try to work logically through your draft from the opening to the closing paragraph.

Voice – Write in an honest and natural tone so the authentic you comes through in your writing.

Your opening paragraph should help clarify your position on your subject and accomplish the following four things:

- It should introduce your subject.
- Gain your reader's attention.
- Identify your thesis or focus.
- Identify the main points you plan to cover.

Open with an engaging story. Provide a dramatic, eye-catching opening statement. Begin with an informative or thoughtful quote. Ask your reader a challenging question. Share some really deep or thought-provoking details about your topic.

Your opening sentences affect the direction and style of your overall paper. If you don't like your 1st, 2nd, or 3rd opening, keep writing. You'll know when it is right because you will be able to visualize your complete draft.

The middle paragraphs in your draft contain the points and supporting details that develop your thesis. In most cases, you should develop each main point in a separate paragraph. Writing that lacks effective supporting details gives only a partial picture. So, let's look at the 3 levels to properly support your thesis:

The First Level is your controlling sentences, which name the topic. For example:

Some states have adopted graduated licensing programs for nursing home administrators.

The Second Level is your clarifying sentences, which support the main point. For example:

Such programs require that new nursing home administrators receive three different types of licenses.

The Third Level is your completing sentences and adds details to complete the point. For example: *First, they must obtain a residency permit, then after six months, an operator's licenses...* and so forth.

Let's look at the key approaches to supporting your thesis:

Explain: Provide important details, examples, and facts.

Narrate: Share a story to clarify an idea.

Describe: Tell in detail how something works or how someone appears.

Define: Clarify the meaning of a specific term or idea.

Argue: Use logic and evidence to support your points.

Compare: Use examples to show how things are alike or different.

Analyze: Examine the parts to better understand the whole.

<u>Reflect</u>: Express your personal thoughts or your feelings about something.

For most papers and longer essays, you should use at least two or three of these methods to support your thesis.

Your closing paragraphs are of critical importance and should do one or more of the following:

- Restate your thesis.
- Answer any remaining questions.
- Review your paper's main points.
- Emphasize the special importance of one of the main points.
- Connect with the reader's experience or life in general.

An effective closing is an ending, plus more for the reader to think about. In the first part of your closing, you want to review the specific points you covered in your paper. In the second part, you want to broaden your scope by saying something more general about the subject, something that will keep the subject alive in the reader's mind.

Revising Your Paper

Revising is the process of improving the thoughts and details that support your messages in your writing. It consists of adding new information, rewriting, eliminating, rearranging, and so forth. Don't pay undue attention to spelling, usage, or grammar early on in this process.

You're ready to revise once you have:

- Completed your first draft.
- Put your draft paper aside for a day or two, and
- Closely reviewed your writing.

First, you should focus on the big picture, your thesis, and the overall organization of your writing.

Then carefully review the specific sections, which should support or develop the thesis.

And remember to version control and backup your work; stuff will happen!

Look at Your Ideas: Make sure you have clearly supported your thesis. Ask yourself this question: Have I answered all of the most important questions about my topic?

Organization: Does your paper flow smoothly and logically from one point to the next? Is your beginning, middle, and end, properly developed?

Voice: Do you convey genuine interest, understanding, passion in your topic? Does the tone of your paper match the purpose (serious, lighthearted, humorous, etc.)?

✓ Verify you have a clear focus.

  ❑ Have you focused on an interesting segment of your topic?

  ❑ Did you express your feelings in your thesis statement?

✓ Verify your writing follows a clear organization.

  ❑ Did you follow a formal method for organizing your ideas?

✓ Do you need to add information?

  ❑ Do you need to make your opening clearer or more interesting?

  ❑ Do you need to add more details to support your thesis?

❑ Do you need to make your closing stronger?

✓ Do you need to delete any information?

❑ Are any of your details redundant or weak?

❑ Do you say too much about one certain idea?

❑ Do any details just not belong?

✓ Do you need to rewrite any parts?

❑ Are some of your ideas unclear?

❑ Do you need to reword any explanations?

Editing and Proof Reading

Editing and proofreading are the line-by-line changes you make to your paper to improve the readability and quality of your paper. Your first concern when editing is to check the style and clarity of your revised writing. Identify any words that sound awkward or out of place. Then you should check your writing for spelling, punctuation, usage, mechanics, and grammar errors.

You're ready to edit once you:

- Complete your major revisions - adding, rewriting, deleting, or rearranging the ideas in your writing.
- Have a clean copy of your revised writing.
- Set your writing aside for a day or two.

Sentence Style: Rewrite any sentences that disrupt the flow of your writing.

Word Choice: Replace any words or phrases that interrupt your tone. Also, replace any overused words or words that lack clarity.

Accuracy: Make sure you follow the standards for spelling, punctuation, grammar, mechanics, and usage. Utilize software like Grammarly to help you achieve correct and accurate copy.

✓ Sentence Structure

- ❑ Did you use clear and concise sentences?

- ❑ Do your sentences flow smoothly?

- ❑ Did you vary sentence lengths and vary your sentence beginnings?

✓ Word Choice and Usage

- ❑ Did you avoid redundancy?

- ❑ Did you use the correct words (their, there, or they're)?

- ❑ Did you use specific nouns, verbs, and modifiers?

✓ Punctuation

- ❑ Does each sentence have the correct end punctuation?

- ❑ Did you use commas and apostrophes correctly?

- ❑ Did you punctuate dialogue correctly?

✓ Capitalization

- ❑ Did you start all your sentences with capital letters?

- ❑ Did you capitalize the proper names of people, places, things, and ideas?

✓ Grammar

- ❑ Do the subjects and verbs agree in all your sentences?

❑ Do the pronouns agree with their antecedents?

❑ Did you use the correct verb tenses?

✓ Spelling

❑ Did you check for spelling errors?

As you can see, quality papers take a lot of work, and preparing your paper a night or two before its due date is a recipe for a poor grade. Follow the guidelines in this book, and you will be well on your way to consistently earning that "A" on all your papers.

Communicating
With Your Professor

Students make all kinds of excuses for not going to see their professors. Some students think they will just be bothering their professor; others are scared to go for any host of reasons. Students don't know what they will say. They think the professor will think they are stupid or think maybe the professor will be mean to them. Often students just don't see any value in meeting with the professor.

Don't be one of those students! You want to build personal relationships with all of your professors. Professors want to make a positive impact on their student's lives. They want nothing more than to contribute to your success. Sure, there are a few of those self-absorbed professors on campus, but they make up the minority.

Think of your professors as your personal advisory board, mentors that can help you achieve your life goals. If you are just going to class, taking notes, turning in your assignments, making good grades, but not building relationships with your professors, you are not getting all you can out of college. A large number of students get scholarships, internships, and job opportunities as a result of a professor referral!

You can talk to your professor about a whole host of topics. You don't have to limit your dialog to the class assignment or lectures. You can and should ask life questions, questions about picking a major, being successful in college, keys to finding jobs after graduation, and such. Questions like: What advice would you give to students who want to be successful in the field of your choice? What made you pick your field of study? What do they wish someone had told you when you were in college, or something they were told, but they wish they took more seriously? What trends do they think will influence the job market most over the next few years? What skills should you pick up outside the classroom to stand out from others? And so on.

Your professors have been where you are, many have been where you want to go. Utilize their help, learn from their journey. Not building relationships with professors is one of the biggest mistakes students make.

How to Email Your Professor

Inevitably, you will have to email your professor. When you do, follow these simple guidelines.

Make sure you spell your professor's name correctly! Almost nothing will make a worse first impression with your professor than spelling your professors' names wrong. Take a moment and verify the correct spelling of their name.

One professor, one email. Please don't send a group email to your professors. Make sure you email them individually. One semester I had a student send a group email to all her professors asking when the final exam was in their class, as her mom wanted to book her travel well in advance so she could save some money. This student decided it was a waste of her time to look at five different course syllabuses or the university website to see her exam schedule, so she thought she would use her professors as her personal assistants. Needless to say, this email approach did not go well. Even if it might be appropriate to email multiple professors, it is almost always better to send an individual email.

Don't address your professors by their first or last name only. Don't use Mr. or Mrs. – The best way to start is with "Dear Professor or Dear Doctor. If you are unsure whether your professor has a Ph.D., just use the title professor.

Make your email subject line clear, specific, and concise. Your professors get a lot of emails, and many of the emails are about how to complete assignments, what was missed in class, excuses for why students weren't in class, and the like. Make your subject line very clear and be concise so your professor can quickly understand the purpose of your email.

Don't ramble on with one huge paragraph. Keep things tight, use only 2-3 sentences per paragraph, and where appropriate, utilize bullet points to make your email easier to follow and much more ascetically appealing to your reader.

Never say urgent, or Please Reply Immediately. This will send your email right to the trash bin or certainly the bottom of the pile. Lack of planning on your part doesn't constitute an emergency on your professors' part. If you waited for an hour before the assignment is due and expect your professor to respond immediately, you would be in trouble. In fact, they are likely to make a special note of your procrastination and grade your assignment accordingly.

When emailing your professors, make sure to identify yourself and your corresponding class information. For instance, Dear Professor Stemmle, this is Sallie Smith from your M, W, F 11:00 a.m. CBAD 350, Section 05 - Marketing class. Your professor has hundreds of students, multiple classes, and sections, and they will greatly appreciate you identifying where you fit in their schedule.

Don't make your professor guess at what you need. You want to clearly state the reason for your email. I am writing to provide you with my doctor's note for missing the test on Monday, and I would like to schedule the makeup exam. I am writing to schedule an appointment during your office hours, or what have you.

You want to make sure your email demonstrates a professional tone and is free from grammatical errors. Don't give your professors a bunch of BS. They have heard it all and know when you are giving them BS, even if you think they don't. Shoot straight and be professional.

Make sure to thank your professor for their time and consideration. And end your email with the salutation of "Best Regards," "Regards," or "Best Wishes."

Following these guidelines will allow your request to be reviewed in the most positive light, and make sure to say thank you, even if you don't get your desired response.

Going to Class Matters

Don't skip class! If you do skip class, don't bother asking for extra time on your assignments or any special accommodations. Professors are very annoyed by students who don't come to class, then want special accommodations, or want the professor to explain assignments they have already gone over in class. Emailing your professor to explain an assignment they have already gone over is not a recipe for success.

Don't make special requests that demonstrate to your professors that their class is not a priority in your life. Life is all about choices, and don't ask your professor to take their time to update you on what happened in class because you overslept, could not find parking on campus, got distracted watching YouTube, or what have you. Don't tell the professor you missed class to pick up your parents at the airport or take a friend to court, and so you now need them to tell you what you missed in class. Make sure you have a few students in each of your classes that you can ask for this type of information.

When you do miss class, don't ask, "Did I miss anything important?" The professor immediately thinks, no, I just wasted everyone's time in class again, like usual! Again, have other student's contact info to see what you missed.

Things You Shouldn't Do

Contrary to popular belief, there really are bad questions. Asking questions that are answered in the syllabus is an example of a bad question, and it demonstrates you are unprepared or lazy.

Don't email to ask when grades will be updated; this may aggravate the professor into spending extra time on your assignment. Professors are notoriously lazy when it comes to grading, don't put the spotlight on yourself by holding them accountable.

Don't ask the professor to explain an assignment or ask when the exam, test, or assignment is due (unless it is not in the syllabus). It is ok to ask for clarification on assignments; just don't ask for an explanation of the entire assignment in front of the entire class.

If you make an appointment to see your professor, show up! If you can't make it, email the professor well ahead of time (24 hours – not 24 minutes). Your professor will be highly annoyed if you blow him or her off.

Don't ask for exceptions, more time, or special consideration in class or in front of other students. The answer will be no. Want an exception or special consideration? Ask in private, don't send an email. Professors at state universities rarely will put exceptions in writing as their emails are discoverable as they are state employees. Best to ask in person.

Don't challenge your grades via email. Instead, ask for help in closing the gap between your actual grade and desired grade. If you challenge a grade, you will almost always lose unless there was a clear mistake made. And you likely will have all your other assignments graded harder. If you got a "B" on your paper, schedule time with your professor to get tips on what you could have done to make an "A." If the professor gave you detailed comments, don't waste their time by asking for a one-on-one review of said comments. The best thing in this situation is to take those comments to heart and meet with the professor before the next paper is due and see if they will provide comments on your rough draft. By doing this, you demonstrate you took their feedback to heart, and you want to learn and improve. It is important to make sure you make any adjustments your professors suggest (don't ignore them because they might seem like a lot of work), and then watch your "A" come rolling in.

You will communicate with your professor in a host of nonverbal ways. First, please don't sit in the back of the class. Professors know that the best student's rarely sit in the back, and like it or not, they will form judgments. You are communicating a lot about yourself, just by where you choose to sit.

Don't spend the class time on your smartphone. Yes, I know student's all around you will be on their phones; just don't be one of them. Professors will feel disrespected if you spend time on your smartphone and will think you really don't care about their class.

Don't spend the class time chatting with your cute neighbor during lectures. If you want to talk up another student, get to class early or hang out after the lecture, college is not high school, and distractions will result in you being asked to leave the class.

Don't show up late to class! Showing up late puts you in a negative spotlight. Sure, coming late is better than not showing up at all, but don't make a habit of it. Parking can be a hassle on most college campuses, but college professors expect you to know this and plan accordingly. Have a finicky alarm on your phone, set a second alarm. Some professors have been known to lock the door once the exam or test starts. Guess what, your tardiness just earned you a zero.

Don't sit in class with your headphones listening to music; this will aggravate your professor to no end. It communicates you have zero respect for what your professor has to say.

Don't blow off a bunch of class assignments, then when you realize you are going to fail, expect the professor to let you turn the assignments in late because you can't just afford to fail the class, lose a scholarship, or what have you. If you do happen to miss one of your assignments, explain to the professor this is not normal for you. Tell them you realize they hear this all the time. Ask them if you can demonstrate that you do high-quality work and turn all your other assignments in on time; will they consider giving you an opportunity to make that one assignment up later.

Don't wait until the last two weeks of class, and ask how you can get your 28 average up to a "C." Professors are very attentive to students during the first 9 or 10 weeks of the semester. After that, there is typically very little they can do to help you out. The key is to communicate with your professor at the first sign you need help, not after you have tanked 50%, 60%, or 75% percent of your grade.

Don't blame your network being down, your computer dying, or your online assignment portal crashing as a reason your assignment is late. Your professors expect you to complete your assignments with enough time to deal with any technical issues you may encounter.

Don't ever tell the professor how busy you are, and that is why you need extra time or missed an assignment. Everybody is busy, and it is completely disrespectful to imply no one else is as busy as you. Everybody has the same 24 hours in the day; you choose what you do with those hours.

NEVER ever sleep in class! You are better off missing class than going to sleep in class. The professor may never notice you weren't in class, but they will definitely notice if you are sleeping in class. If you happen to doze off, apologize to the professor right after class.

Don't tell the professor you really need an "A" in their class. They care what grade you earn, not what grade you need. And don't say you will do anything for an "A" or to pass the class! Your professor thinks, "Anything," I guess, anything but what you needed to be doing all semester!

Don't ask to take your exam early because you have a cruise planned to Cancun over spring break or a ski trip to Aspen over winter break. Professors expect you to plan your trips and vacations around your schoolwork, not the other way around.

Don't tell the professor you don't understand how your paper got a "C" as this paper made an "A" in another class or, worse yet, at another university!

Don't miss a bunch of classes for no reason, and then tell the professor your class schedule prevents you from coming by during their office hours. Your professor thinks… really because you seem to have no problem blowing off my class on a regular basis.

Don't go over the professor's head. You may feel inclined to speak to the department chair or even the dean about an issue you have with your professor, don't do it. Work it out with your professor. If you can't work it out with your professor, ask your professor if he or she can set something up with the department chair.

If you still have issues, I don't recommend going to the Dean; instead, seek out your office of student advocates for council and advice. They typically will get the Dean involved if needed, and this is a much more effective approach to reaching a resolution. In all your dialogs, it is important to remember not to personally attack the professor but instead target the actions you are objecting to or have an issue with. You don't want to attack the individual; you want to address the situation.

Things You Should Do

Now that I have talked about the things you should not be doing, it is time to talk about the things you should be doing.

You want to demonstrate you are serious about the class; you want to be attentive and demonstrate you enjoy your professor's lectures. Basically, you want to show respect and engagement by attending class, being on time, participating in class discussions, asking good questions, sitting up front, and demonstrating you are listening via your nonverbal body language. Smile, nod your head up and down, laugh at the dumb jokes, and what have you.

Asking great questions is really a good way to connect with your professors. Can you ask a question that ties a previous lecture into the current class discussion? Professors love when you listen and remember prior points or concepts they have gone over in their class lectures. Ask your professor's opinion about a current happening in the field or a topic tied to their research interest.

Visit your professors during office hours. I can't stress enough just how important building a relationship with each professor is to your success. Let them know just how much you enjoy their class and how it is making a positive impact on your life. Professors really do want to make an impact; let them know they are!

Managing Your GPA

I am surprised by the number of students that believe GPA is not especially important to their future success. These students somehow believe that the best employers just want students with a degree. They mistakenly think employers will somehow magically see their GPA is not a reflection of who they really are, what they are truly capable of. They believe that somehow companies will look past their poor GPA and will realize their true untapped potential.

When I ask a student how they will ever get a chance to convince an employer of their potential when their GPA will not even meet the threshold for them to even apply, they are quite lost at that point! They don't realize that many companies and positions will require a student to have a 3.0 or 3.5 GPA to even apply for a position.

I want you to think of the workplace like a pyramid. At the bottom of the pyramid are all the struggling companies. And as you go up the pyramid, there are better companies, but less of them. At the top of the pyramid are the world-class companies, your Amazon's, Google's, Facebook's, and such. There are very few great companies out there! And do you think those great companies hire "C" students from "C" universities as a normal course of business? Of course, they don't!

Many students ask me, but after my first job, GPA will not matter, right? Well, yes and no! It is true that GPA will matter less and less once you gain more experience, but students with the best GPAs tend to get the best opportunities, they get the best experiences earlier, and it can take quite a few years for you to recover from a slow start and poor GPA.

As an example, in a recent study of third-year financial analysts, the study reported that a 3rd-year analyst made an average total annual compensation of about $65,000 if the person's GPA was 2.8 or less. This compares to $77,700 for a GPA of 2.9 to 3.1. The "A" student, with a GPA of 3.8 to 4.0, pulled down an average total compensation of $115,700, a more than $50,000 a year premium over the 2.8 or lower graduate.

Even when you enter a field with a fixed pay structure or strict starting salary guidelines, such as becoming a teacher or educator in the public school system, your GPA is going to significantly influence the hiring decision. Do parents and school districts want "A" students or "C" students teaching their children?

The Harsh Reality Is C's may get degrees, but A's and B's succeed earlier!

- A low GPA could damage your income for years!
- A low GPA could make it more difficult to land an internship!
- A low GPA could jeopardize scholarships and financial aid!
- A Low GPA could make it more difficult to launch a great career!
- A low GPA could limit your graduate school opportunities.

Now that you understand how important GPA is to your future, let's jump right in and look at some of the basic things you need to know about GPA, and then we will get into the specifics on how to maximize your GPA to set you up to have the success you deserve!

GPA is the benchmark used to evaluate your performance in college! It is also the benchmark those in a hiring position will use to filter out recent college graduates to determine which candidates will enter the interviewing process. Is it the only criteria? Of course not, but it is typically a requirement that you obtain a minimum GPA of some level to enter the interview process. Typically, companies set the threshold at 3.0 or 3.5 for a student to even be considered for a position.

But why do employers place so much emphasis on GPA? Your GPA reflects your ability to plan, organize, focus, work on deadlines, and drive results. In this case, your grades demonstrate all these things to your future employer. It isn't a perfect proxy for how you will perform in the workforce, but if there is a better one, it hasn't been discovered yet. You see, in college, you are given assignments to complete, guidelines to follow, and those assignments receive grades. This is a lot like how a job works! So obviously, employers will use your GPA as a predictor of your performance if they hire you. Given that your GPA is so important, we obviously need to spend some time tracking and managing our GPA. Let's take a look at how GPA works at universities.

In the same way that your professors and instructors give you a grade to evaluate your progress or success in their particular course, your Grade Point Average is similarly a score used to evaluate your success during the entirety of your degree program.

Here is how it works. Each course taught is given a certain number of "units" or "credits," depending on the content of the course. Most college courses have a course load of three units (approximately three hours of lecture per week), but the weights can vary from 1-course hour to more than 5-course hours.

GPA typically assumes a base grading scale of A, B, C, D, F. Each letter grade is assigned a number of grade points. An A grade receives 4 points, a B=3, a C=2, a D=1, and an F=0. Additionally, some universities will work on a plus or plus/minus system. For example, a "B" would receive 3 points, and a "B+" would receive 3.5 points.

If you take a three-unit class and receive an "A" grade, you receive 3 units times 4 points (for the "A"), which gives you a total of 12-grade points for the course. Let's say you also take a 4-unit class (common in a science course, for example) and receive a "C" grade. That's 4 units times 2 points(for the "C") for a total of 8 points. So, for your two classes, you have collected 20-grade points for the 7 units.

To get your overall GPA, you then divide the accumulated grade points by the number of units. In this case, the math is (20/7=2.86), so your GPA is 2.86, which is slightly less than a "B" average.

A quick word on percentages versus GPA points. In College, a Final Grade of 90% is the same as 100%. You will be awarded a GPA of 4.0 regardless of your individual percentage grade. An 80% carries the same weight as an 85%. Many colleges use a plus or minus system to differentiate grades just a little bit more. For instance, an 80 would be a "B" and be awarded 3 GPA Points, while an 87 would be a "B+" and receive 3.5-grade points. That extra ½ point can make a major difference in your cumulative GPA.

At most universities, you must maintain a 2.0 GPA to be in good standing. If your GPA drops below that threshold, your school will place you on what is called academic probation. You may be required to take a specific class designed to improve your academic skills, you may need to attend tutoring sessions, and you may be required to check in with your academic advisor on a regular schedule.

Along related lines, you may need to keep your GPA at or above a certain level to keep your scholarships, financial awards, or loan eligibility. Being on academic probation is no fun and comes with a lot of additional stress and commitments. Failure to remove yourself from academic probation in a timely manner can mark the end of your academic career at your current institution.

Students quickly learn that most financial aid and scholarship money come with GPA requirements. And academic probation is not only stressful, but it is also expensive and may even make college unaffordable altogether.

Additionally, you will find that opportunities for special programs, academic honors, research, internships, department scholarships, and some core classes all come with GPA requirements.

It's always a smart idea to review GPA requirements with your academic adviser and office of student financial aid for your specific requirements. You don't want to find out you're in trouble after it's too late to recover.

Making the Dean's List or President's list is a difficult and prestigious accomplishment. Many universities lower the threshold for Dean's List for their Freshman from the typical 3.5 GPA to a 3.25 GPA. You want to understand what your university requirements are for Dean's List so you can set your goals appropriately. President's list is typically an honor reserved for those students that earn a 4.0 GPA.

After your first semester, you are making a first impression before you even walk into the class! Make it a good one! Most universities use online learning management systems such as WebAdvisor, where faculty and students manage their courses, check financial status, report grades, etc. As part of these systems, faculty can see which students have been on the Dean's List, Presidents List, Academic Probation, are repeating the class, etc. So yes, you are actually making the first impression before you even walk into the class for the first time!

Paying attention in class takes effort; it's hard work. By sitting in the front of the class, you force yourself to pay attention; you position yourself in the area where there are fewer distractions, and subsequently, you perform better and earn a higher GPA.

Now even if you sit in front of the class, you still need to ensure you come to class. I can tell you that students who come to class make significantly better grades. Research has shown that a student who attends only a quarter of the lectures on average earns a 1.79 (D+), while a student who attends all of the lectures on average earns a 3.44, just shy of a "B+". Attendance alone accounts for 31 percent of a student's variance in performance. Going to class is one of the easiest ways to boost your GPA!

While in class, how you take notes actually impacts your GPA. Study after study supports that students who handwrite their notes have a stronger conceptual understanding and are more successful in applying and integrating the lecture material than those who took their notes on their laptops.

Taking your notes by hand forces the brain to engage in some heavy "mental lifting," and these efforts nurture comprehension and retention. By contrast, when typing their notes, students can easily produce a written record of the lecture without processing the actual meaning, as faster typing speeds allow students to document a lecture without devoting much thought to the content itself.

Students who utilize laptops for their notetaking tend to take notes in a fairly mindless fashion. This method of typing your notes leaves little room for analysis or synthesis by the brain. This kind of mindless notetaking fails to promote any real or meaningful understanding of the application of the information. When college students use their laptops, they spend some 40% of their class time using applications unrelated to their classwork, are more likely to fall off task, and are less satisfied with their education. In one study, nearly 90% of laptop users engaged in online activities unrelated to coursework for at least five minutes, and roughly 60% were distracted for half the class.

Laptop use in the class decreases course grades by over 1/3 of a grade point. And when you factor in writing your notes, the latter is some 30% more effective than taking notes on your laptop. Bringing your computer to class is just not a recipe for success.

This next one will likely surprise you. Sleep may impact your college grades more than drinking or drugs. For each night that college students have sleep problems, the lost sleep was associated with a 0.02-point drop in their cumulative grade point average (GPA)

116

and 10 percent higher odds that they would drop a course. Lack of sleep and pulling all-nighters are almost a rite of passage on a college campus, but the reality is, lack of sleep can significantly impact your GPA.

Too much alcohol will have a detrimental impact on your GPA. Research shows a definite link between the number of binge drinking episodes and grade-point average—the students who abused alcohol more frequently have lower GPAs.

Greater frequencies of alcohol abuse were linked directly with lower GPAs. Students who had two incidents of binge drinking in a month had a 3.06 GPA; those with 3 to 5 incidents, 3.04; those with 6 to 9 incidents, 2.98; and those with 10 or more incidents, 2.95.

The studies defined binge drinking as five or more drinks in a row (for males) or four or more drinks in a row (for females). A drink was defined as a bottle of beer, a glass of wine, a wine cooler, a shot glass of liquor, or a mixed drink.

Even where you live impacts your GPA. Research has found that living in campus housing contributes to better student academic performance, higher retention, and higher graduation rates. Students who live on campus their first year also have higher GPAs and retention rates.

Students who live off-campus are nearly twice as likely to get a GPA below 1.0 as those living on campus. In addition, those living on-campus have an average GPA that is anywhere from .19 to .97 points higher than their off-campus counterparts.

Living on campus is not just good for your GPA; it also provides you opportunities to meet new people and develop new friendships and participate in social and recreational opportunities that are more convenient.

Working while going to school may or may not impact your GPA. Researchers for the Bureau of Labor Statistics found that students who worked less than 20 hours per week had an average GPA of 3.13, while non-working students had an average GPA of 3.04.

Students working a moderate number of hours a week has actually shown to help students perform better in the classroom. Working too much has been shown to have negative effects. The Bureau of Labor research shows that students who worked more than 20 hours a week had much lower grade point averages, 2.95 on average.

It makes logical sense that working too many hours each week could negatively impact a student's grades. When work becomes more than a part-time priority, students can begin to have trouble managing their class load.

Contrary to most popular wisdom, students who register for more credits tend to earn higher GPAs and have greater retention even after controlling for academic ability, prior academic success, on-campus employment hours, and other background characteristics. Students with higher workloads are often more focused and manage their time better as they have little time for distractions.

Students who register for what is considered your more difficult courses, however, tend to earn lower GPAs and experience lower retention. The results are consistent regardless of student's prior academic performance.

College students are receiving at least partially incorrect advice. If students wish to maximize their GPA and increase their probability of retention, they should be taking heavier first semester and first-year credit loads. Heavier credit loads may force students to manage their time more effectively or acknowledge that academics is a full-time job. In turn, coming to terms with time management or recognizing that academics is a top priority may result in not just coping with a few more credits but may result in raising their overall level of academic performance.

Exam schedules can also have a big impact on your GPA. Having two or three exams on the same day can be a real detriment to your GPA! Most universities will allow you to reschedule an exam if you have three exams on the same day but two exams on the same day, and you are out of luck. Since final exams can be 50% of your grade, having to face two exams on the same day could be a big issue. Universities post their class exam schedule on their website, so when choosing your class schedule, be aware of the exam times for your classes. Indifferent between two classes? Take the class that will give you the most prep time for all your finals.

The days of the week you take your classes can also impact your GPA. For some classes, you might not have a choice when you can take the class (if calculus is only taught on MWF in the afternoon, you have no choice but to do it on MWF in the afternoon or not take calculus at all)

Now, if you say, need to choose between two classes for an elective and your decision really is down to the TTH or MWF sections, you want to pick the class that balances your overall schedule.

Most students find the schedule that provides them the most balance is three classes on MWF and two classes on TTH. This allows you to spread out your efforts, attention, and assignments in a more consistent manner.

Although research seems to suggest that classes meeting three days a week are more effective than those meeting one or two days a week, conflicting research suggests that the most commonly skipped classes occur on Fridays.

Some research has argued that the dropout rate and nonfailing rate is higher in classes with more frequent meetings. Regardless of the day of the week that you take your classes, balance the gaps in your schedule. If you can take your three MWF classes back-to-back, you have a long block of uninterrupted time for study, work, and fun. Long blocks of time between classes make it harder to manage your time and increases the likelihood you might blow off a class.

Not only the day of the week but the time of your classes can impact your GPA. Most research has found time-of-day does play a significant part in student achievement. Many studies have shown that the lion's share of students perform better in reading during afternoon hours and mathematics during morning hours. Every effort should be made to align your class schedules to meet your specific learning and energy cycles.

The high school you attended will also impact your GPA. In accounting for both first semester and first-year GPAs, students from larger high schools tended to earn higher GPAs. You can't change the high school you went to, but if you went to a small school, you want to prepare mentally for the challenge ahead, recognizing that students from larger schools may have a head start on you.

Choosing the right electives will impact your GPA. Every college has electives that are easier than others. Students often ask if they should take an easy elective class to boost their GPA or take a class that is harder but may help them with their future careers.

I would like to tell you to always take the course that will help your career, but that would be irresponsible. Sometimes you need to take an easy class to get those GPA points, and that is just a reality of college life. You may have to maintain your scholarship, you may need to get off academic probation, you may need to reach a threshold GPA to apply for that internship or job. Sometimes you do need to manage your GPA by taking a "fluff" course.

Strategically dropping classes can boost your GPA. Too many students are hesitant to drop a class; in fact, many parents do their students a disservice by encouraging them to stick with their schedule, work harder, and don't quit. Parents mean well, but more frequently, exercising your option to drop courses is a better strategy. Many universities offer what is called repeat forgiveness. If your university has this type of program, you can gamble and stay with a class longer and see if you can pull it out. Repeat forgiveness allows you to retake a class and replace your grade from your previous attempt. If you do drop a class, make sure you understand the impact on any scholarships or financial aid.

One difficult course can derail other classes. Many of the courses students struggle with include math, statistics, and the like, and these courses all build on the beginning foundational concepts. When students find themselves behind, it is very difficult to catch up, they get overwhelmed, and then one difficult course can start to impact their other courses as they lean into their struggling class. Students need to evaluate whether trying to recover their grades in one class will negatively impact their other courses and, subsequently, their overall GPA.

With all that said, make sure you know your universities drop policies. Many universities let you drop as many classes as you want. Other universities limit the number of classes you can drop in your academic career. Make sure you know your university limits, drop dates, and policies.

It is important to understand that your GPA is an output; it is the result of all the effort you put in over the course of each semester and, ultimately, your college career. To effectively manage your GPA, you must effectively manage yourself.

Attending class, actively listening, taking notes, doing your assignments, preparing properly for your exams, getting help when you need it are the key inputs that drive your grades and, ultimately, your GPA. Take care of the inputs, and your GPA will take care of itself.

Prioritization is another important tool in successfully managing your GPA. Prioritize your 4-credit hour course over your 3, 2, and 1 credit hour courses. A four-credit hour course counts 4x more toward your GPA when compared to a 1-hour lab. You simply just can't put in the same amount of time in a 1-hour course as you do a 3- or 4-hour course. Prioritize your work based on its overall impact on GPA! I am not saying a 1-hour course is not important; it is! But when your back is up against the wall, focus on impact.

I have mentioned that not all professors have the same focus, but other variables come into play. One big complaint students have is that some professors are just harder to understand than others. Build a network of students and be sure to ask other students for their feedback on professors to take and professors to avoid. If that fails, search online websites for professor reviews. Do all you can to know about the professor before you sign up for their class.

One of the best things you can do to improve your GPA is to hang out with other students with the same academic goals as you, those that have their priorities in line, and those who can help you succeed.

Form a study group for the classes you find difficult and look for stronger students to join the group. A study group can be a complete waste of time if you spend all your time explaining to your slacking roommate how to do everything!

Balance is important, and you don't want to load your schedule with too many difficult classes in the same semester. If you know Calculus will kick your butt, try to take easier classes to balance your workload. But sometimes, there will be no way around it. If you do have to take difficult classes in the same semester, try to balance them in your schedule, so they are on different days, and if you have to take them on the same day, try not to take them back to back. A break in between will give you an opportunity to refocus and prepare.

Managing your GPA is an important responsibility for you, one you can't take lightly. Make sure you have a specific GPA goal for each semester. I encourage all students to strive for a 3.5 GPA or higher. Many jobs will require a 3.0 GPA or even a 3.5 GPA to even apply. And if you do graduate with a 3.7 GPA or higher, you will find you have separated yourself from the masses.

When it comes to managing your GPA, regardless of your goals, it is critical that you remember to get help early, actively manage your schedule, do your own research, know your university rules, and drop classes when appropriate.

Goal Setting

If you want to achieve something in college or in life, the preliminary step is to decide what that is! By setting goals, you state what you are seeking to attain. It defines how you want to see yourself for the next four years and beyond. Goals may pertain to any aspect of your life like college, financial stability and security, fitness, career, or hobbies, etc.

Practically all of us have goals we want to reach, but many of us struggle with how to reach those goals and how to turn our goals into reality. Sometimes, it's not easy to figure out how to get started in reaching those goals, letting the obstacles that stand in our way block us from reaching our goals.

The key to achieving the most you can out of college and life is to turn your goals into your reality. Most times, the loftiest goals that seem impossible to reach are much more achievable than we first think. We just have to break these seemingly impossible goals into small doable steps. Once we breakdown any lofty goal into more manageable steps, we quickly realize our goals are achievable.

In this book, I will show you why it is so important to set goals. You will learn how to properly set goals by utilizing the SMART goal methodology. You will also gain an understanding of the differences between your short-term and long-term goals and how they support each other. You'll also learn why it's important to write your goals down. To reach goals, you have to first define them, then prioritize them so that you can reach all of your goals in the most efficient manner possible. In addition, you'll discover why you need to set specific deadlines for your goals. Plus, you'll learn how to overcome and eliminate distractions that will stand in your way of achieving your goals. And finally, you will learn how to track your progress so that you can better manage and overcome distractions so you can achieve more of the goals that you set.

Setting a goal is like having a personal map, a compass, and a clear route to your destination. You know where you are and where you are heading. To achieve your goals, you first have to have goals. It's a lot like driving to a destination; if you don't know where you are going, how are you going to get there? Therefore, you need to set goals in life for things you want to achieve.

Many people who have goals are not consistent in their approach to setting them. This is a mistake because, if you aren't consistent in your goal setting approach, then you can wander around aimlessly in your actions, believing that you are getting closer to the goals you want when in reality, you are wasting time and energy that could be better utilized if you set proper goals ahead of time.

This is why proper goal setting is so important. Many goals that seem like they might be impossible to achieve on the surface are actually quite achievable when you actually set the goal utilizing the SMART goal methodology.

If you are wanting to get a college degree in a specific field but have never taken a college course before, you may think you don't have what it takes to get that degree. Yet, if you really set the goal of attaining that degree and break down the steps needed to attain that degree, you'll see that you are fully capable of attaining that degree by following the steps and actions outlined by your university. Yes, you will have challenging classes. Yes, you will have setbacks. But you will take things semester by semester. You will put in the time and effort, and before you know it, you will have that degree.

Too many students enter college without clear goals, or they simply have the goal to do the best they can or maybe to simply graduate. Setting the goal to do the best you can is a trap. It is not specific, and it is not measurable, and certainly won't inspire you when things get a little tough, which they will.

Effective goals are what we call SMART goals. They are specific, measurable, attainable, relevant, and timely. Let's look at each one of these individual components.

Specific

Each goal needs to be clear and specific. When your goal is clear and specific, you are able to focus your efforts and feel truly motivated to achieve it. Your goals should be well defined and clear to anyone that has a basic knowledge of your goal. When drafting your goal, you need to be able to answer the five "W" questions:

- What do I want to accomplish? For instance, I want to make at least a 3.5 GPA my first year and graduate in 4-years with at least a 3.7 GPA.
- Why is this goal important? I want to get a job with a world-class company, and I need a good GPA to make that happen.
- Who is involved? My professors, advisors, parents, study cohort, and of course, myself.

- Where is it located? The university you are attending.
- Which resources or limits are involved? Scholarships, student loans, support from my parents.

Measurable

Your goal must be measurable to enable you to track your progress and stay motivated. Assessing progress helps you to stay focused, allows you to meet your deadlines, and also provides the excitement of knowing you are getting close to achieving that all-important goal. A measurable goal should address questions such as:

- How much? What will cost me to complete my degree?
- How long? How many years will it take me to graduate?
- How will I know when my goal is accomplished? Final GPA and Graduation Date.

Achievable

Achievable goals are realistic and attainable goals. In other words, the goal you have set should stretch your abilities but still remain achievable. Experts suggest you should set a goal that you have an 80% chance of achieving. The 80% threshold challenges you but does not demotivate you because your goal seems impossible or just too difficult. When you set goals that are achievable, you are able to identify previously missed opportunities or tools that can accelerate your achievement.

An achievable goal will answer questions like:

- How can I accomplish this goal? I will go to every class, get a class or two ahead, do all the prework, and if I run into any problems, I will head immediately to the tutoring center, form a study group, etc.
- How realistic is the goal, based on other constraints, such as financial factors? I am lucky I do not have to work a job, so

college will be my full-time job and primary focus. I will manage my distractions and approach college with 100% effort. If you have a job, are a student-athlete, or have special constraints on your time, you want to identify those commitments. Once identified, you can develop realistic goals based on your individual circumstances.

Relevant & Realistic

This step is about ensuring that your goal matters to you and that it also aligns with other relevant goals you have. The goals need to be important to you, not because your mom and dad told you, not because a teacher told you, but because you want to achieve them.

We all need support and assistance in achieving our goals, but it's important that we retain control over them. So, make sure that your goals drive you forward as you are ultimately responsible for achieving your own goals. A relevant and realistic goal will answer "yes" to these questions:

- Does this action seem worthwhile?
- Is this the right time to start?
- Does this match my other efforts/needs?
- Is this aligned with who I want to become?
- Will this create a better future for me?
- Do I have the ability to make it happen?

Time-bound

Every goal needs a deadline. This allows you to focus on your activities required to achieve your goal and gives you something to work toward. This element of the SMART goal criteria helps to prevent daily tasks from taking priority over your longer-term goals.

You want to ensure you have enough time to achieve the goal, but not too much time that could result in completely diluting your goal.

Someday is not a day of the week! A well written, time-bound goal will usually answer these questions:

- When?
- What can I do 4 years from now?
- What can I do a year from now?
- What can I do 16 weeks from now?
- What can I do this month?
- What can I do this week?
- What can I do today?

Our current actions impact our future results, so we have to make sure we understand how our short-term and long-term goals connect and support each other.

When most people set goals, they think in their minds of a goal they want to achieve, then go about attempting to achieve it. But, you really need to analyze the goal to see how you can break it down into more manageable and more easily attainable parts (i.e., short-term goals) so that you can attain the ultimate goal (i.e., long-term goals) you want. That process is much more effective when you are writing things down.

You may be asking yourself, "Why do I need to write down the goal? I know what my goal is." You may already know what your goals are, but the problem is that, by just having your goals in your mind and not writing them down, you can more easily make excuses on why you are not making as much progress toward your goal. You can even persuade yourself that certain actions you're taking are helping you to reach your goal when, in reality, they aren't really doing anything to help you reach it.

Additionally, the very act of writing down a goal helps you actually commit to it. Write down your goals on a piece of paper and put it in a visible spot in your dorm room, that piece of paper is always right there, reminding you of what your goal is. You constantly see it, and your mind is immediately reminded of the goal you set, giving yourself a boost of motivation and determination to redouble your efforts to achieve that goal.

Writing things down is powerful on two levels: these are called external storage and encoding. With external storage, you're storing the information contained in your goal in a location (e.g., a piece of paper) that is very easy to access and review at any time. It doesn't require a neuroscientist to know you will focus on something much better if you're staring at a visual cue every single day.

But there's another deeper phenomenon happening, and it is called encoding. Encoding is our biological process by which the things we perceive make it to our brain and get processed. From there, our brains make a decision on what ultimately it will store in our long-term memory and, subsequently, what it will discard. Writing has been proven to improve the encoding process. In other words, when you write things down, it has a much greater chance of being remembered and feeling real.

People who write their goals down are 1.2 to 1.4 times more likely to successfully achieve their goals than those people who don't write their goals down. That really is a big difference in goal achievement just from writing them on a piece of paper.

You need to define your specific goals so you can improve your odds of success. Just as you have to decide where you are going in an automobile before you can get there, similarly, you have to decide what goals you want to achieve before you can actually achieve them.

A goal is your desired result or achievement that you desire to reach. Therefore, you need to decide what you want to achieve in your life. You need to decide what you want to be remembered for and what actions in your life you want to do to reach this goal. In determining the goals, you want to accomplish, ask yourself what really drives you, what motivates you to get up in the morning.

Does helping your family matter a lot to you? Is developing a successful career matter to you? Are you driven by protecting and saving the planet? Are you wealth driven? Is it something else entirely? You need to decide what really matters to you, then decide what you want to achieve to accomplish that desire. If the environment is important to you, maybe you want to earn a degree in a field related to protecting the environment? Maybe your goal will be to start your career with a company that is focused on protecting the environment? Maybe you want to start your own company whose mission is to protect the planet.

Once you know what drives you and what matters to you, you'll have a better idea of what goals you want to achieve in your lifetime. Then, you can break down those goals into more manageable and attainable tasks and short-term goals to make the long-term goals more easily attainable.

Prioritizing your goals is important for many reasons. For one reason, we all have a finite lifespan; none of us live forever. Therefore, we only have a limited time to accomplish everything we want to achieve. It is vital that we prioritize our goals so that we achieve the goals we want to achieve as early as possible since we are not guaranteed the opportunity to reach them later in our lives.

Another reason to prioritize our goals relates back to the idea of short-term goals and long-term goals. With most long-term goals, there are many short-term goals we can and need to reach before we can accomplish the long-term goal. As a result, we need to prioritize the short-term goals first because we will need to reach our short-term goals before we can obtain our long-term goals.

We want the long-term goals the most, but they are virtually unattainable if we don't accomplish the short-term goals first. If we want to lose 100 pounds, it will be impossible to just focus on that goal without recognizing and achieving the short-term goal of losing 5 pounds first, then losing 5 more pounds, and so on.

Similarly, we can't attain a college degree if we don't first get into college; we have to pass high school and get a good score on our ACT or SAT test before we have the chance to earn a college degree. Therefore, you have to prioritize the goals you want to achieve. You can't graduate college if you can't get into college in the first place.

First, you only have a limited amount of time to achieve the goals you want to achieve. Second, to attain the long-term goals we most want to achieve, we have to achieve many short-term goals first. This will take you some time and a committed effort to achieve. Therefore, it's important we prioritize the goals we want to attain so that every action we take can bring us closer to your short-term goals and, subsequently, the long-term goals we want to achieve. You can think of short-term goals as the individual steps you have to climb to reach your long-term goals.

Even the best-laid plans can go astray if you get distracted from the task at hand. Everyone will face distractions, and you will have to learn to limit their impact. Whether it's internal distractions, such as having doubts about completing tasks or losing focus during a task, or external distractions, like social media. Unexpected circumstances will pop up, everyone has to learn to manage distractions on their way to achieving goals. One of the keys to successfully achieving your goals is to consistently overcome and eliminate the distractions that stand in your way.

If you are looking to earn a college degree in four years' time, you have to stay focused on the coursework you need to complete in order to achieve that degree in the allotted time span. This means you must be willing to take the correct course load, complete the assignments and study for the exams needed to successfully pass the courses, even when your family wants to spend time with you or your friends want to go and party, etc. If you allow distractions to interfere with your studies, you may fail the course and prevent yourself from earning that degree in the time span you want to attain it in.

If you find you are routinely distracted by email or social media, log out of those while you are completing your work, put your phone in a drawer, so it is out of sight so that you are not distracted again. If your family or friends are providing distractions, ask them to not disturb you while you are studying unless, of course, there is an emergency or maybe move to another location for more effective studying and more timely completion of your work.

When you do get off track, keep notes of those times, and look for any commonalities. Is one particular friend constantly derailing you? Is your roommate distracting you every Friday night? By tracking your shortcomings, you will be more prepared in the future and be well on your way to achieving your goals!

Goals are the things that move us forward in our lives. Goals are the oxygen that fuels our dreams. They are the first steps to every journey we take and are also our last. So, it's very important that you realize the significance and importance of goal setting and apply this knowledge in your life.

When you take the time to set and prioritize your goals, you ensure that your life is focused on getting the most out of your college experience. There is so much to do and experience in life, but many of the things we want to achieve, and experience will not be handed to us; we need to work for it.

In this book, you have learned the importance of goal setting in order to achieve your goals. You have learned the differences between short-term and long-term goals and how these goals interrelate with each other. You have also learned why writing down goals is so important in order to achieve them. Most successful people write down the goals they want to achieve because writing it down commits you to it, plus it's always right there for you to look at, reminding one's mind to redouble your efforts to attain the goal you want to achieve.

You also learned why you need to define and prioritize your goals. You have to define goals in order to know what tasks to do to achieve them, much like you have to decide upon a destination when you are driving an automobile. You also have to prioritize your goals in order to achieve as many goals as possible. Your lifespan is not unlimited, and if you come down with a critical injury and/or disease/condition, you may not be able to achieve the goals you want to achieve after that point. Therefore, it is vital that you prioritize the goals you want to achieve to ensure you get as many completed as soon as possible.

You've also learned why setting a specific goal deadline is key. Most long-term goals can be broken down into various stages of tasks, each of which can be labeled as a short-term goal. By having long-term goals serving as your compass, you can insert short-term goals as interim steps to ensure you stay on track to achieve the long-term goals on schedule. Failure to finish the short-term goals in the time spans you have indicated will likely jeopardize your ability to attain your long-term goal in the time span you have established.

You learned about how to overcome and eliminate distractions that stand in the way of your goals. Everyone has to deal with various distractions when working to achieve goals. If you're looking to lose 30 pounds in 12 months, allowing yourself to eat rich, nutrition-deficient foods will only hamper your progress toward achieving that long-term goal. If you're looking to earn a college degree in four years, losing focus and getting distracted will lead to you doing poorly on your homework and exams, leading to you failing the coursework and ultimately failing to attain your goal to complete your college degree in four years.

You need to track your progress each day in terms of the goals you want to complete. By estimating how much you believe you should get done each day, then comparing how much you actually get done, you can see how productive you have been and what is causing you to be less productive.

Picking A Major

For many students, picking a major seems like a life-or-death decision! Let me put you right at ease here. According to a recent study, only 27% of people end up working in a job closely related to their major. Surprisingly, about 30 to 50 percent of students in the United States end up changing their major at least once. The reality is, at 18-20 years old, how could you possibly be expected to know what you want to do for the rest of your life? With that said, let's dive deeper into the whole major topic.

Should You Apply With a Declared Major?

If you're applying undeclared because you're unsure about what you want to study, that is perfectly fine! Studies have shown that applying to college undeclared does not have a negative impact on a student's chances of being admitted.

However, if you do know what you want to study, applying undeclared is not generally a good strategy. The idea of applying without declaring a major is that you have time to explore and try different areas of study. However, this is not without some downside.

The downside is that you will not be able to take advantage of some major-specific classes, mentorship programs, outside activities, or internship opportunities that are available to those students that have declared a major.

At most universities, you're not guaranteed a spot in your desired major unless you actually applied and were accepted under that major. The process of changing majors can be difficult; some schools have a separate process for students wanting to change majors. If your major is especially competitive, the process might be extremely bureaucratic and difficult.

If you have a competitive major you want to apply for, but your high school performance may not be up to par, you can use the first year of college to build a strong GPA. If this is the case, it might make sense to apply as an undeclared student.

There are some situations in which it may benefit you to declare your major on your college application. If your major requires a specific curriculum starting in your freshman year, then it is certainly in your best interest to declare your major.

Applying to college with a specific declared major may also allow you to qualify for additional financial aid such as department-specific scholarships, special freshman housing, or professional development opportunities that are only available to declared students.

The bottom line is this; take a look at your individual situation, your university policies, and make the decision that works best for your needs.

Declaring a major is a rite of passage during college. You will eventually need to declare a major, typically before you start your junior year. The time to make your major decision will come quicker than you think, but you do have two solid years to explore your options.

Students who have not yet decided or declared their major can still enter their junior year. The issue is that your classes at this level are major-specific, and you will likely be adding additional semesters to your college career if you have not decided.

I always recommended that students declare a major by junior year, even if they are still uncertain. Remember, only 27% of people end up working in a job closely related to their major, so take your best guess and just get on with it.

Choosing a college major was difficult enough back in your parent's day when there was only a handful of majors for them to choose from. Today, there are hundreds of majors you can choose from.

The good news is it is not as complex as it may first appear. All these hundreds of different college majors typically fall into six categories. At first glance, it could seem to be an impossible task to sort through hundreds of different possibilities, but don't panic; by focusing on six general categories, you can narrow down your search. Let's look at the core six:

- Arts-Related Majors.
- Business-Related Majors.
- Environment-Related Majors.
- Engineering and Technology Majors.
- Science and Math-Related Majors.
- Literature, Language, and Social Science Majors.

Are you good with numbers? Are you creative, are you more visual? Do you want to work outside? Do you love social media? Do you like to work with teams? Do you like to build things? Do you like to manage things? Do you like to teach people? Finding a major that aligns with your personality and interests is the key to happiness and success.

Sometimes, we know more about what we don't want as opposed to what we do want. Hate math? Don't have an artistic bone in your body? Well, you just eliminate two of the six categories. Sometimes by eliminating the things we don't like, we can narrow our options down to discover the things we will like.

I am amazed at the number of students who pick a major that they have no real aptitude for. They picked their major because the job outlook was good, they heard they could make good money in the field, or maybe they are following in the footsteps of their parents.

Please don't do that! Take the time to explore different options. Do you enjoy social media, are you creative, do you enjoy helping people share their messages? A major in digital marketing may make all the sense in the world for you. Do you like numbers, enjoy creating and building things? Maybe architecture is your path. Love investing and all things related to the stock market? Enjoy helping other people achieve their financial goals? Maybe wealth management is in your future.

Take the time you need to try out some different classes to gain new experiences, and you will be in a good position to make your decision. Success is most often found at the intersection of your talents and your passions, so take the time to find your passion. When you pick your major, you are choosing the initial direction you will be launching your career from. You might even follow that path for a big part of your career. That's why it's important to find something you are passionate about.

I recommend students take an elective class that is outside their comfort zone. This approach will help you dive into areas you never knew you might enjoy but could end up being exactly what gets you excited. Of course, you'll also want to consider other factors that will impact your future. Many folks are burdened financially and most realistically balance their passions with the practical realities of paying the bills. If you are unsure of the topic of jobs you might enjoy, take a strengths finder test. This test will give you insights into where your abilities and interests align.

Unfortunately, I see so many students give up on their dreams at 18 or 19 years old! It really does break my heart. I hear things like, "I wanted to be a nurse, a doctor, an engineer, but those majors are just too hard." Too hard! Just wait until you experience your future at a job you don't like for a decade or two. You will learn the meaning of hard!

Now is the time in your life to challenge yourself, to grow, to work hard, and make the sacrifices, so you can benefit from all your hard work for the rest of your life.

Success has a compounding effect, just like earning interest on your money. Do the hard work now, so things will be easier in the future. If you goof off at this point in your life, you will face decades of hard consequences. Challenge yourself now, test yourself, find out just how good you can be!

Some majors require an advanced degree to significantly increase your odds of getting a job and having a fulfilling career. Majoring in psychology? You most likely will need a master's degree or Ph.D. to pursue many of the most rewarding positions. Studying Economics? You likely will need a Ph.D. for the majority of the jobs in that field. Studying management? Well, you will be competing with those who have years of work experience as well as others with MBAs.

One exercise I make my students do is to pretend they are graduating in 30 days and find 7 to 10 jobs they would be interested in applying for and look to see what the requirements are for those jobs.

Take those jobs and identify the skills gap you have, and work to close that gap as you head toward graduation. Do all the jobs you like require a master's degree? Do the jobs you like require specific technical skills like SQL? Do they require internship experience? Certain certifications? The key is to develop a roadmap, so when graduation does come, you are in the best position to launch your career.

One of the best ways to determine if a particular major is for you is to talk to other students in that major already. Learn why they picked their major, what they like, and dislike about their majors. Ask them what things they wish they knew back when they were earlier in their journey.

Ask them about their internships, clubs they participated in, professors they really liked, and the professors they didn't care for too much. Ask them to describe the challenges and opportunities. By talking to students who are already well down the path you are considering, you can gain valuable insights and knowledge.

Should I Pick a Minor?

What is a minor? Think of it as a mini-major. Minors are obtained by focusing your optional classes on a specific track or minor (usually four to six upper-level classes).

I am often asked, "Should I pick up a minor," and my answers range from yes to no to maybe. The first question I ask is, "What are you trying to accomplish by picking up a minor?" You need to make sure you have a clear vision of how a minor will help you achieve your goals.

Sometimes, you can pick up a minor without having to pick up any additional classes. If you plan far enough ahead, fitting a minor into your overall degree while meeting your core requirements is entirely possible. However, in many cases, a minor is just more effort and cost than it's really worth. Rarely is adding a minor worth extending your graduation another semester.

Taking on the challenge of a minor can be very useful if it complements your major. Say you're a digital marketing major, and you pick up a minor in data analytics. A big part of marketing is analytics. A minor in data analytics can give you an edge. Maybe you're a computer science major, a minor in business could help you show that not only can you code, but you have an understanding of the business side as well. A minor can show that you are strategic, determined, and take the initiative.

A minor won't cover up any of your shortcomings in your overall academic performance, and many hiring managers will not place much weight on your minor versus your major, so if you are going to tackle a minor, make sure you are doing it for the right reasons.

Maintain a Healthy Perspective

Research shows, 62% of recent college graduates are working in jobs that require a degree, yet only 27% of college graduates are working in a job that closely relates to their major.

I don't want to totally downplay or disregard the impact of a major on your future earnings potential. There is no question that certain majors pay significantly more than other majors. I am just saying that your major doesn't pigeonhole you into a particular job or field for life.

Some majors do pay more than others. For instance, Counseling and Psychology majors make an average of $29,000 per year, compared to $120,000 for Petroleum Engineering majors. That's a difference of 314 percent or $4.1 million over a 45-year lifetime of work.

Another example is the difference between two popular majors, General Business and Elementary Education. A General Business major earns $60,000 annually, compared with $40,000 for an Education major. Over a lifetime, that's a difference in earnings of about $900,000.

If you want to be an accountant, architect, engineer, doctor, attorney, etc., your major can obviously have a significant impact on your ability to pursue those professions. But as your career develops, your experience is what people will be evaluating. Too many students just don't take advantage of the opportunities they have in college to network, get involved in student clubs or organizations, and volunteer for causes they are passionate about. These types of activities reflect well on your resume; they tell employers that you are passionate, motivated, and focused.

Employers want to ensure that you are a quick learner, will fit into the workplace environment, and will be able to execute the job requirements. A recent survey of businesses shows that some 93% of companies believe that your critical thinking, communication, and problem-solving skills are more important than a job applicant major.

A whopping 95% of employers are looking for candidates whose skills translate into their ability to demonstrate out-of-the-box thinking and demonstrate creativity and innovation. So many of today's best jobs are rapidly changing, utilize more technology, and require a foundation of continuous learning to be successful.

One thing I recommend my students do is to listen to a lot of podcasts. Say you are a business major, but you have no real idea what you want to do in the field of business. Head over to iTunes and find the top-ranked podcast in business. Listen to podcasts on marketing, management, entrepreneurship, management, leadership, and so on. Find a topic that resonates with you, then dig deeper. Read some books, blog posts, research papers on the topic, see if you are still interested. Listening to different podcasts is a great way to uncover passions and interests you never knew you had.

Another method to find your path is to conduct informational interviews with people working in the field. Reach out to individuals on LinkedIn whose jobs seem interesting to you, tell them you are a

141

college student working on picking your major, and you would like to talk to them for 15-20 minutes, finding out what their day looks like and gain a little insight into their profession.

If any informational interviews go well, ask if you can shadow them in their job for a day or two. Job shadowing is a terrific way to gain insights into the type of work you would be doing in the future.

Head over to www.getmyfreebookresources.com, and I will send you a list of questions that you can ask during your informational interviews to help make sure you get the most out of your interview.

Build Your Network

The network you build in college may matter way more than your college major. One area that students often need to shift their perspective on is the topic of networking. Networking is truly critical to those who want to be successful, and you should put in just as much work into your networking during your college career as you do your academic studies.

You should start your networking as soon as you hit campus, start by building relationships with your professors, academic advisors, other students, and by setting a weekly goal of new connections to create on professional social media sites like LinkedIn. Your network can be an especially important source of mentorship and play a pivotal role in helping you discover your major, not to mention a source for internships and career opportunities.

Volunteering can be more productive than an actual internship in figuring out what you might want to do. Charities have the same needs as for-profit businesses, and they always seem to need help with everything from marketing to event organization to, well, you name it. Most recruiters surveyed placed volunteer experience on par with work experience. Volunteering will allow you to build your network and gain practical insights into a career.

The key idea is to continually try things that will give you new experiences. You won't find your passion sitting on your couch, playing Fortnite with all your free time. The key here is to get out there and keep trying new things!

If You Fall Behind

Sometimes, despite our best efforts, we will find ourselves lost. Maybe you did not do your prep work. Maybe you just are having trouble grasping a particular concept. Regardless of the reasons, when you find yourself lost, you need to address it immediately.

First off, don't panic and don't get frustrated. You have to keep a positive mental outlook and not let the stress of the situation overtake you; that will just start a negative cycle that will be harder to break. Remind yourself that you have been lost before, and things have worked out, and they will work out again.

Take a step back, pause, and start over with a fresh perspective. Sometimes starting over again will give you the time to see things you didn't see before. If you are lost during the lecture, don't check out, stay focused, and do your best to capture the main ideas and points the professor is making.

Head over to the tutoring center while things are fresh in your mind. If you are still having trouble, make an appointment to see your professor and get things cleared up. Don't wait until right before your exam to try and figure things out.

Ok, you thought you had it down, but you were wrong. You bombed the exam, what do you do now? Don't miss the test debrief. Your first goal now is to figure out what you missed, what went wrong. In college, things build on each other, so your first goal is to learn what you did not learn. If your professor doesn't do an exam debrief, make an appointment with your professor or their teaching assistant and make sure you understand where you went wrong. Too many students just quit when they get a bad grade. They chalk it up to experience and tell themselves they will do better the next time. Don't do that. Commit to learning what you missed.

Next, you want to figure out what went wrong in the first place. You want to make sure you change your preparation prior to the next exam. Did you miss too many of your classes? Did you fail to capture important details? Did you fail to answer the right questions? Did you focus on the wrong things? Figure out what went wrong so it doesn't happen again.

Assess the real damage. Is your exam 5% of your grade or 50% of your grade? What percentage of your grade is still available to earn! Do you have 95% of your grade still out there, 5%, or some percentage in between? Obviously, the more of your grade already earned, the less opportunity you have to recover. If your midterm was 50% of your grade and you totally tanked it, it may make total sense to drop the class.

I hear students say things like the class average was a 65, so my 67 was not really that bad. Yes, it was! Regardless of how the majority of students did, there is usually a handful of students that always do well. You want to be in that handful. Process all the feedback you can, and learn from that feedback, and build it into your plan going forward. Let's look at what you can do if you are in trouble or headed for trouble.

Extra Credit Assignment

Request an extra credit assignment. Don't do this in class or by email. Make the request in private face-to-face. Explain to the professor the reasons for your shortcomings and ask if you can

144

complete an extra assignment, do some research on a project they are working on, or some other project for extra credit.

Ask for an Extension

What if my assignment I have to turn in is crap? Ask for an extension! Again, do this face-to-face and in private. You have nothing to lose to ask for an extension on an assignment or ask if you could redo your assignment for some extra points, etc. Don't "cry a river" just explain that due to some difficult circumstances, you have not been able to do your best work, and you would like to know if there is anything you can do to help recover the situation.

Timing Matters

Please don't wait until the majority of the semester is over to ask for help. This aggravates the heck out of professors. You want to address any issue you are facing immediately and before the drop date. Most professors are much more willing to work with you in the first half of the semester, as opposed to the back half.

Strategically Dropping a Class

Sometimes it may take so much effort to recover in one class, it will negatively impact your grades in your other classes. Dropping a class to reduce your workload and allowing you to perform better in your other classes may make sense. Sometimes you just have too much on your plate, and you need to get a few things off it.

Loans May be a Better Choice Than Work

Taking out student loans instead of working may be a very smart option. I know this is not popular advice, but if you are struggling, lose the job and focus on your GPA. Graduating is your first goal and graduating with the highest possible GPA is right there near the top of the list. Landing that great job because you had a high GPA will more than make up for the lost money from that minimum wage job.

145

Prioritization is Needed

Lastly, adjust your priorities. If you are not doing well, you need to eliminate everything that is taking time away from your studies or distracting you. You need to double down your academic efforts and finish strong.

If you are pulling a 2 point something in most of your classes, you really might be in trouble. In college, a "C" is not a good grade! If you are missing assignments, asking for exceptions, or turning in subpar work, you are heading for real trouble.

If you are struggling to understand the main points of your professor's lectures, you might be in trouble. Most students get lost from time to time, but if you are struggling to follow the majority of the lectures, you are likely in real trouble.

If you are struggling to get through your foundational Math and English courses or even taking multiple attempts to pass those classes, you need to focus on building your base academic skills.

College can be stressful. Especially as you adjust to college, having to tackle new courses, mid-terms, and being on your own. However, if you are stressed out every week, not sleeping, not eating, feeling depressed, you need to seek help and evaluate your current path.

College can be demanding, but if you are spending sunup to sundown doing nothing but your course work, you really should evaluate if your current college is the best fit for you. I am all for going to the best college you can get into, but research shows if you can't academically perform in the top 20% of your class, you likely are better off at a less demanding university. I want your college experience to be well rounded and balanced; it should be enjoyable. Remember, you want to be challenged, not continually overwhelmed.

I Am In Deep, What Do I Do Now?

So, you recognize you are heading for trouble, or you are already deep in those troubled waters. What do I do now?

You have to take a step back, take a deep breath, and relax. Many students are overwhelmed. They question their academic abilities, they have let their health and wellness decline, their relationships are stressed, it seems like their whole life is out of control.

The first thing we must do is properly identify the problem, the true root cause of your issues. If your mental health is in question, please make sure you seek counseling and support. You need to make sure your well-being is taken care of before anything else.

With that said, to recover from being in trouble, you need to identify what got you there in the first place. What were the key underlying causes that led you to this situation? Did you miss a bunch of classes? Did you not turn your assignments in? Did you procrastinate and wait until the last minute on everything? Were you dealing with a difficult life issue? Did you not take everything seriously enough? Did high school not prepare you for the academic challenges of college? Did you have to work too many hours? Were you partying too much? Were you just distracted all the time? Often, many students' problems stem from a single root cause or bad habit.

Next, you want to determine if your problems are really solvable! Sometimes you will have no choice and you will have to take your medicine. Actions have consequences, and if you have dug yourself into a hole, you may have no choice but to drop a class or two. But what if all your classes are a disaster? In that case, talk to your advisor about a "semester withdraw." Yes, that is an expensive and extreme approach, but it beats the heck out of failing out.

If depression is a problem, seek counseling, see a medical doctor. If you are just too challenged academically, look into transferring to another school.

Meet with your professors to see if the math can work? If you are failing, but 75% of your grade is still to be earned, you probably can recover. If you are failing and 50% or more of your grade is already earned, you likely are in real trouble. Even if you can partially recover with, a "C", will you create a new problem like losing scholarships that requires a "B" average?

Develop a plan, but don't develop a plan alone. Universities invest a significant amount of time, energy, and resources to ensure student success. Work with your professors, advisors, counselors, doctors, tutoring resources, writing labs, parents, classmates, etc., to help develop a recovery plan. Sometimes that may require seeking professional help and needing to put college on hold. Other times, it may just require a moderate course correction in your habits and approaches.

Don't play the victim card. You are responsible for the situation you find yourself in. Go ahead and own it, lose the excuses, and accept where you are.

Work on your plan. Your best chance at recovering is to take action and execute your plan. Your plan probably isn't going to be 100% correct. You may be in deep, but regardless, adopt your best course of action and go to work on your plan. Don't look back, don't beat yourself up for getting yourself into this position, don't feel sorry for yourself, just work your plan to the best of your ability.

But What if Things Don't Work Out?

In life, you will face many setbacks, things that often don't work out as we initially plan. Learn from the experience and start again more intelligently with the lessons you have learned. Failing a class is not the end of the world. Finding yourself on academic probation is not the end of the world. Failing out of college is not the end of the world. Quitting, giving up, well, that certainly can be the end of the future you dreamed of.

If things don't go your way, get up, dust yourself off, and try again, this time more intelligently, more focused, more motivated, and more disciplined. Just don't give up on your dreams!

Learning Styles

The traditional view on intelligence has been that intelligence is something you were born with. It was thought that you only had a finite amount of it, and tests could tell you how smart you are. The theory of multiple intelligences challenges that view. In short, this theory states that each person has different ways of learning and uses different types of intelligence in their daily lives.

The theory of multiple intelligences separates intelligence into individual modalities. It doesn't see intelligence as something that is dominated by a single general ability. While some students can learn very well in a linguistically based environment (reading and writing), others are better taught through mathematical-logic based learning. Still, others benefit most from body-kinesthetic intelligence (learning by doing with the hands).

Each of us possesses some of each learning style to an extent, but there is always a primary, or more dominant, processing method. I will discuss the four primary learning styles, along with the eight different forms of intelligence. Understanding how you best process information and learn is the first step in maximizing your academic planning and performance.

Let's look at each of the different types of learning styles. The term "learning styles" recognizes that all students effectively learn differently. Theoretically, an individual's learning style refers to the preferential way each student absorbs, processes, comprehends, and retains information. In other words, everyone is different. By understanding what kind of learner, you are, you can get a better perspective on how to implement more effective and efficient plans and study techniques. There are four basic ways people learn, so let's take a look at each.

Visual Learning

The first style is Visual Learning. Visual learners absorb and recall information best by seeing. These students learn best through graphic representations that explain what could have been said in normal text format.

Aural Learning or Auditory Learning

Studies show that auditory learners learn their best while they are engage in active listening. Auditory learners find conventional study practices, such as the practice of note-taking from their textbook, not all that effective. They much prefer to ingest information through audio or video clips or by discussing a topic.

Read/Write Learning

This type of learner is someone who requires reading and/or writing down the information to learn it. They absorb and retain the most information through reading and writing text, versus the use of imagery or symbols.

Kinesthetic or Tactile Learning

Kinesthetic Learning is a learning style in which learning takes place by the students carrying out physical activities rather than listening to a lecture or watching demonstrations. The Kinesthetic learner learns by doing hands-on, direct involvement.

These four different types of learning styles are represented by the acronym VARK or Visual, Auditory, Reading/Writing Preference, and Kinesthetic learning. The VARK model clearly acknowledges that students have different preferred approaches to how they process information, referred to as "preferred learning modes."

In a typical classroom for every 30 students: 17 students would be multimodal (~60%)

- 6 students would be kinesthetic.
- 5 students would be read/write.
- 1 student would be visual.
- 1 student would be aural.

Don't get caught up in thinking one learning style is better; there is no right or wrong learning style. VARK is about how you perceive and process information the best! You are capable of learning by any of these approaches. The VARK just shows your preferences, your preferred way of perceiving, and processing information.

So, just what is intelligence? Simply defined, intelligence is the ability to acquire and apply knowledge and skills.

The standard psychological view of intellect states that there is a single intelligence, adequately measured by IQ or other short answer tests.

Multiple intelligences (MI) theory, on the other hand, states that human beings have several relatively discrete intellectual capacities. There are several components of this multiple intelligences theory and they are: Logical/Mathematical, Visual/Spatial, Bodily/Kinesthetic, Musical/Rhythmic, the Naturalist, Interpersonal, Intrapersonal, and Verbal/Linguistic.

151

Are you someone who can remember names but not faces? Or maybe you remember faces and not names. Maybe you can remember numbers for exams, but geographical locations can't be recalled easily. Maybe you can remember every word to your favorite song, but not the periodic table. The Theory of Multiple Intelligences may explain why.

Think about your own behavior during high school. If your teachers use their linguistic intelligence to teach, as is the case in most classrooms, and your intelligence is not well suited for this approach, did you get frustrated? Zone out? Instead of focusing on the lecture, did you find yourself fidgeting (Bodily-Kinesthetic), did you start to doodle (spatial), maybe even started chatting up your neighbor (interpersonal)?

To be successful in a lecture environment, you are going to have to translate your professor's information into your own personal intelligence, just as you would a foreign language.

Let's look at each of the different types of learning styles to understand their key tendencies, and then we will go into tips on how you can optimize your academic strategies based on your individual strengths and weaknesses.

First, let's look at the traits of Verbal/Linguistic Intelligence.

- Listens and responds to the spoken word.
- Enjoys reading, writing, and discussing.
- Remembers what has been said.
- Remembers what has been read.
- Speaks and writes effectively.
- Easily learns other languages.

Logical-Mathematical Intelligence

- Extremely comfortable with concepts like quantity, time, and cause and effect.
- Like to use abstract symbols to represent concrete concepts.
- Enjoys math and using technology to solve complex problems.
- Often gravitate toward careers such as accounting, computer technology, and law.

Bodily/Kinesthetic Intelligence

- Prefer touching, handling, or manipulating learning lessons.
- Highly developed coordination and a keen sense of timing.
- They learn best by direct involvement and participation.
- Clearly remember what was done, rather than what was said or observed.
- Favor concrete learning experiences such as field trips, building models, role-playing games, or physical exercise.
- Often will have great skills in acting, athletics, and dance.

Visual-Spatial Intelligence

- Learn most efficiently while they are seeing and observing.
- They are great at recognizing faces. They also clearly grasp objects, shapes, colors, details, and scenes.
- Think in pictures and visualizes detail.
- Recall information best when using visual images as an aid.
- Enjoy the arts and objects in visible form.

Musical Intelligence

- Listens and responds with interest to a variety of different sounds, including the human voice, environmental sounds, and music, and organizes such sounds into meaningful patterns.

- They are eager to be around music and learn from music and musicians.
- Develops the ability to sing and/or play an instrument.

Interpersonal Intelligence

- Bonds with parents and interacts well with other people.
- Develop and maintains strong social relationships.
- They are highly focused on other people's feelings, thoughts, motivations, behaviors, and lifestyles of others.
- Expresses an interest in interpersonally oriented careers such as teaching, social work, counseling, management, or politics.
- Is aware of their range of emotions.
- Is motivated to identify and pursue goals.
- Works well independently.
- Establishes and lives by an ethical value system.
- Strives for self-actualization.

Naturalist Intelligence

Naturalistic intelligence is a person's interest in and relationship with the natural world of animals, plants, and the natural world around them.

- They recognize and can name many different types of trees, flowers, and plants.
- They have an interest in and good knowledge of how the body works and keeps abreast of health issues.
- Are conscious of tracks, nests, and wildlife on a walk and can "read" weather signs very well.
- They have an understanding of, and interest in, the main global environmental issues.

Study Tips

Ok, now that we know some of the characteristics of the various intelligence, let's look at how we can approach our academic studies to get the most bang for our intelligence styles. Remember, although we all have a preferred method of learning, try incorporating ideas from other learning styles to augment your studying and break up the grind.

Verbal/Linguistic Study Tips

- Rewrite your class notes.
- Record yourself reading your class notes and try playing the recording as you study.
- Paraphrase what you have heard.
- Develop questions, find the answers, and speak them out loud.
- Discuss what you are studying with others.
- Ask a lot of questions.
- Read aloud dramatically, perhaps even with an accent and use lecture recording or record and listen to notes as you read.

Logical/Mathematical Study Tips

- Create hypothetical conceptual problems to solve.
- List your key learning concepts in a logical and numbered sequence.
- Analyze how the textbook chapter is organized and why.
- Build a flow chart or diagram that communicates what you are learning in a logical step-by-step fashion.

Bodily/Kinesthetic Study Tips

- Act out or role-play the material you need to learn.
- Practice a skill as soon as it is learned via hands-on experience.
- Walk around while you are reading.

- Listen to audio while you are exercising.
- Take notes on postcards and then arrange the topics so that they make better sense to you or make new relationships.
- Make notes by paraphrasing the material instead of just taking notes on what the author or teacher is saying.
- Reflect on the information while you take a walk or go do something else.
- Use a friend or study group to help you study.

Visual/Spatial Study Tips

- Create a learning map using keywords and nouns.
- Show your notes by drawing diagrams and charts.
- Mark up your textbook to show relationships among concepts.
- Create a poster, cartoon, video, or timeline.
- Use symbols instead of words.

The visual-spatial learner generally thinks in visual pictures rather than using word representation. They also like to learn holistically, instead of sequentially, or in parts. As such, learning maps are a great tool for any visual learner. A learning map is a graphic representation that highlights the knowledge, skills, and big ideas that students should get from a lecture or assignment. The map illustrates the most important information that needs to be learned and how the individual chunks of information are connected.

The visual-spatial learner is astute at seeing the big picture of things but can easily miss out on the details. As such, you want to:

- Highlight new ideas with a highlighter.
- Write down the details, not just the big ideas for what you hear.
- Prepare graphs and diagrams to reinforce the details.

Musical Study Tips

- Write a song, jingle, or rap from your study materials.
- Play music in the background as you think about the topic, ideas, and lessons.
- Classical music has been shown to actually stimulate the emotional center of the brain.
- Sing or hum as you do your work.
- Some find that playing a single song on repeat allows them to hyper-focus.

Interpersonal Study Tips

- Discuss the topic and ideas you need to learn.
- Teach what you are learning to someone else.
- Compare your notes with another student taking the course.
- Keep track of your personal reactions to course material.
- Make a personal connection with ideas or concepts.
- Study alone and engage in internal dialog about the course content.
- Try to determine why it matters to you and how you can use the information.

Naturalist Study Tips

- Seek out applications of course content in the natural world.
- Study outside when the weather permits.
- Find a physical location that exemplifies course material (for example, the beach for your marine science class).
- Look for the applicable environmental implications of what you are learning.

Become a Multi-Sensory Learner

You can increase your intelligence by developing your multi-sensory study skills; studies have shown that we remember 20% of what we read, 30% of what we hear, 40% of what we see, 50% of what we say, and 60% of what we do. Of course, this varies from person-to-person depending on their learning preferences. So, if you can activate your seeing, hearing, and doing during your studying, your ability to remember and recall information will go up several hundred percentage points. If you:

- Read and visualize the material; you have seen it.
- Read key points out loud, makeup questions, and answer them; you have heard it.
- Write out the answer to your question and circle the major point. You have done it.

The point here is to do something extra that helps you learn using multiple senses.

Personality Tests

A personality test will give you detailed insights into your distinct personality traits. Your personality will have a significant influence on the relationships with those around you and will even influence your overall health and well-being.

My favorite quick and easy personality test is the True Colors Personality Test. This personality test asks you a series of questions designed to rate your likes and dislikes. The test will then classify your personality as a color, either a blue, green, orange, or gold personality type. Many people are a combination of two colors, but usually, a student will exhibit one primary color.

The true colors personality test is a great way of understanding yourself and understanding others. Everyone has some degree of each color, but one color is predominant.

Personality tests can help you as a student by increasing your productivity, helping you get along better with classmates in study groups, helping you to realize your full potential, and identify learning strategies that are most effective for you.

You should realize that your personality type is not about what you can do. It's about what you prefer to do!

Grab a pen and sheet of paper for a very quick exercise. I want you to simply draw two straight lines about 5 inches long, one right above the other, leaving about a ½ inch or so between the lines on your paper.

Now on the first line, write your name. Now put your pen in your other hand and write your name on the second line.

What was different the second time around? For most people, the second attempt takes a lot longer, is messier, probably feels strange, and requires more concentration.

But could you do it? Of course, it's just that you prefer doing it the first way! The first way is easier and more natural; the second way makes a simple task seem like hard work. In college, you are going to have to learn "writing with your other hand," or simply doing things that don't come naturally.

I have discussed the various learning styles, types of intelligence, and personalities. Simply knowing about these concepts is good, but it's important to go further and act on that knowledge. The way to maximize your efforts as a student is to find ways to translate from your professor's preferences into your own preferences.

We that said, we need to focus on making strategic choices. First, lean into your strengths, become the best learner you can be at what you're naturally good at, but also realize that you'll need to become more versatile over time. In your career, you will not always be able to choose what you do and how you do it, so best to start working on elevating your weaknesses now.

It is important to realize that no one can learn for you, just as no one can eat for you. You will have to do the work. Don't fall victim to making excuses! The, I could have been more successful in college if, "If I hadn't had to work so many hours," "If my roommates weren't such a bad influence," "If, If, If!" Don't walk away from college with a bunch of Ifs! Give it your best every day!

Listening

Listening is one of the most important skills we can develop in college to be successful. Without good listening skills, you can't take good notes, you can't prepare properly for assignments and exams, and your GPA will be impacted. In a nutshell, you will struggle to reach your full potential in college.

But listening isn't as simple as it seems. It is a process. The listening process is made up of five stages: receiving, understanding, evaluating, remembering, and responding. A good listener must hear and identify the words that are being said, understand the meaning of those words, critically evaluate or assess the message, remember what's been said, and respond to or record the information they have received.

But before we jump into the individual stages of listening, it is important to understand that we receive our messages on three basic levels: Vocabulary, Voice inflections, and Non-verbal behaviors. Vocabulary messages consist of the actual words we are using to communicate with others. Voice inflections consist of the way that someone says something. This would include tone, speed, emotions, pace, and volume. The way someone says something can dramatically change the meaning of the words being spoken.

There is an old corny joke, my grandfather told me when I was a kid. He said an old Italian guy is swimming on a private beach, and the police show up and ask him if he saw the private beach sign. The old man said the sign stated it was not a private beach. The police read the sign to him, "Private Beach No Swimming Allowed." The old Italian man said, well, I didn't read it that way. The police were baffled and said, how else can you read it. The old man said, "Private Beach? NO! Swimming Allowed." While this might be viewed as more of a punctuation or grammar issue, it does serve to highlight the point, even if it is a corny one.

We also have to understand nonverbal behaviors, including body language, facial expressions, and of course, other gestures that people use while communicating.

Now, when I ask students what percentage of our communication do you think is verbal? I typically get answers like... 70%, 80%, or even 90%. Most students are shocked to learn that only 7% of what we communicate is based on the words or vocabulary. 38% of what we communicate is based on voice inflections, and the other 55% of what we communicate is based on nonverbal behaviors.

Professors often use voice inflections to make points of emphasis, and these can be difficult to detect in the rear of the room. They may make a facial expression to indicate something is important. They may smile as a clue that you may want to remember this point for the exam.

You want to make sure you sit in your class or lecture hall at the proper location to optimize your ability to process your professor's communication on all three levels. Data shows your GPA depends on it!

The Challenges of Receiving Communication

As listeners, we have a lot coming at us. We are bombarded with a variety of stimuli at the same time, so we have to learn to differentiate which of those stimuli are important and relevant.

Effective listening involves being able to focus on what is important while ignoring other distractions. For instance, a student hears the professor's voice and understands that the professor is speaking, then deciphers what the professor is saying despite other stimuli going on in the room. Another example is the challenge of trying to listen to a classmate tell a story while walking down a loud hallway, while your phone is giving you alerts, and you are thinking, do I have time for a quick snack before my next class?

Students may also struggle to effectively receive their professor's communication due to what is known as "speech segmentation." Speech segmentation is a significant component of learning any language, as you have to separate the words to make sense of what people are saying. The words may not connect in a manner you are used to; they may use words slightly out of the normal context. This can often cause barriers in the classroom when a professor's native language is different than the student's native language.

For example, I remember in my stats class in graduate school, an international student asked this question of the professor: In your first example, you said "if we flip a coin;" in your second example, "you said if we toss a coin," I am struggling to understand the difference in the problem examples.

The Receiving Stage

Listening is an active process that must construct meaning from both verbal and nonverbal messages being sent to us. The receiving stage actually has two parts, hearing and attending.

Hearing is a physiological process of receiving sound waves as they hit the eardrum. Obviously, we must first be able to physically hear what we're supposed to be receiving. The clearer the sound, the simpler the listening process becomes.

Along with hearing, attending is the second half of the receiving stage. Attending is defined as the process of accurately identifying and interpreting particular sounds we hear as words. The sounds we hear basically only have meaning when we give them their meaning in context.

The Understanding Stage

The next stage in the listening process is called the understanding stage. Sometimes, you might hear this stager referred to as the comprehension stage. Understanding or comprehension is simply "the shared meaning between parties communicating."

In this stage, the listener must determine the context and meanings of the words that are heard. They will determine the context and meaning of individual words they are hearing and assigning their meaning. This is essential in order to understand a speaker's message. Once you understand the speaker's key point, you can start to categorize the rest of the information you are hearing and organize your mental outline.

Before getting the big picture, it can be difficult to understand and focus on what the speaker is saying. Think about walking into a lecture a few minutes late. You will have no problem hearing the words and sentences that are being spoken, but you may not understand what the professor's point is or whether what you're hearing at the moment is really important, or a simple side note or a big digression.

One strategy you can use to improve your understanding of what your professor is saying is to ask questions. Asking questions allows you to fill in any gaps you may have in the construction of the professor's message.

The Evaluating Stage

This stage of the listening process is where the listener assesses the information they received. We do this by applying both a qualitative and a quantitative filter. Evaluating is the process that allows us to develop an opinion on what we have heard and allows us to start to develop a response if it is needed.

During the evaluating stage, we determine if the information we have heard and understood from the speaker is well constructed or if it is disorganized, is it true or false, is it significant or trivial, biased or unbiased, and is it complete or missing key points.

We also start to determine how and why the speaker has come up with and conveyed the message that is being sent. This may involve considerations of the class objectives, your professor's passions, motivations, and goals.

The evaluating stage occurs most effectively once you fully understand what the speaker is trying to say. While we form opinions of information and ideas that we often don't fully understand, or even that we misunderstand, doing so is not a good practice in the classroom.

Having a clear understanding of your professor's message allows you to evaluate that message without getting bogged down in ambiguities, trivial points, or spending unnecessary time and energy on tangential points.

This is one reason for doing the prework for your class is so important. It gives you a proper foundation and filters to evaluate what your professor is communicating. It helps you identify areas where you will want to pay close attention, ask a question, and ensure you fully understand the key concepts.

You want to head into each lecture with an active game plan. You don't want to be on your heels in a complete reactionary mode.

By combining your prework with your professor's lecture, you can reflect and engage at a higher level with the material. You can process the lecture in terms of how the information affects your own understandings, ideas, actions, and beliefs.

The Responding Stage

The responding stage is the step of the listening process, where the listener provides verbal and/or nonverbal responses based on their recall.

Following the recall stage, a listener will respond to what they hear using either verbal or non-verbal cues or both. Common nonverbal cues include hand gestures, nodding, making eye contact, fidgeting, a cocking of your head, smiling, and even rolling eyes. These kinds of responses occur at both the concise and unconcise level. Nonverbal responses allow the listener to communicate their level of interest without interrupting the speaker.

When someone listening responds verbally to what they hear, with a question or a comment, the flow of the conversation is interrupted, and the speaker/listener roles are reversed. In class, your professor is looking for verbal and nonverbal responses from students to determine how their message is being processed.

Based on student responses, the professor can choose to either adjust or continue with the delivery of their lecture. If students are smiling and nodding or asking questions, the professor will feel like the students are engaged, and their message is being communicated effectively.

The Remembering Stage

The remembering stage is where you categorize and retain the information you have received from the speaker for future use.

We depend on our memory throughout the entire listening process. We actually depend on our memory to fill in the blanks when we're listening and to let us place what we're currently hearing in the context of what we've heard before. Our memory allows us to understand what we are currently hearing in a much broader context.

In listening to a lecture about procrastination, for example, a listener might make a mental connection to a previous time in their life when procrastination caused stress or anxiety.

If we can apply information quickly after receiving it, it will improve the rate of retention and reduce the rate at which we can no longer recall information in our memory. Conversely, our retention is lessened when we don't focus, engage in mindless listening, and make little effort to understand what a speaker is saying.

Because of breakdowns in the listening process, the speaker and the listener may come away with anything from slightly different to completely different meanings to the same communication. In fact, research shows that immediately after a 10-minute presentation, a normal listener can recall only 50% of the information presented. After 48 hours, the recall level drops to 25%.

Many students think they are bad test takers when, in fact, they are bad listeners. They failed to differentiate between important and tangential topics; they failed to absorb a key point. And if they are good listeners, they are likely bad note-takers, relying on their memory when it comes time to prepare for a test. Become a good listener, a good note-taker, and watch how quickly you become a good test taker. Let's look at some common problems you will likely encounter during your college career.

It is important you identify any of these types of issues in the first couple of days of class while you have the opportunity to drop/add and remove yourself from the situation. However, the reality is that dropping and adding is often not an option due to class availability, your work schedule, or a host of other potential reasons.

One problem you likely will incur is the professor who speaks too fast. When you have a professor, who speaks like they are in a race, you must ratchet up your preparation. The more you are familiar with the class material, the easier it will be for you to process what the professor is saying.

The next thing you need to do is partner up with other students and exchange class notes to fill in any gaps you have. Students tend to miss classes, so teaming up with three or four students should ensure you are covered.

Go visit your professor during their office hours to fill in areas where you missed some details or didn't quite follow the point all the way to its conclusion. Don't assume you will figure it out on your own, and don't wait until after you failed a test or bombed an assignment.

But what about just asking the professor to slow down? You can try that in a very polite manner, of course, but habits like speaking fast are hard to break!

You could ask the professor if you can record the lecture, but many professors frown on that. They feel it will reduce engagement with students who are already nervous about participating, or they may just not want their lectures recorded for a host of other reasons.

What if your instructor has a heavy accent? This is a normal occurrence at many universities, especially if your university is a researched focused university.

In this instance, you want to sit as close to the professor as possible so you can see their lips moving. In these situations, preparation is critical so you can make connections between what the professor appears to be saying and what he or she is presenting on the board or screen. Make sure to ask questions anytime you don't understand.

But the real secret sauce is to talk to your professor as much as you can, before class, during class, after class, and during office hours. The more you speak with the professor, the more you will start to understand your professor's accent.

What if your professor is quite a talker? In this case, sit as close to the instructor as possible and try to hold eye contact as best you can. Don't be afraid to bring this issue up with the professor. Professors teach in different size rooms, lecture halls and even teach a wide array of classes. It may be that the professor is just not used to the room your class is held in, and they will make adjustments once they are aware.

You may find out you are sitting next to Chatty Cathy. As students tend to find their way to the same seats in each class, students often feel uncomfortable changing where they sit, don't be uncomfortable, just move!

But what if you try these techniques and you are still struggling? Well, you need to seriously consider dropping the class prior to the withdraw with an "F" date. By dropping the class prior to this date, you are able to drop the class with no impact on your GPA. Some universities limit the number of drops you can make, so you want to understand all of your university policies around dropping classes. Make sure that you meet with your academic advisor to explore and understand all your options.

Are you hesitant about asking questions in class? Do you think that your classmates or professor will think you are stupid? Many students often feel this way, but let me assure you, if you ask questions correctly, your peers and professor will actually be impressed.

There are a few basic steps to asking great questions, and you will quickly be able to adjust your approach to get your question answered and, at the same time, communicate to the professor you value their course—a true Win/Win.

The first step is to be prepared. Doing your prework for your class or lab will help you identify areas you are struggling with and will help you organize and frame questions ahead of time. If the professor clears things up, great. If not, your question has been well thought out and organized.

We keep coming back to this one, sit near the front of the class. Sitting in front of the class makes it easier for you to make eye contact with the professor as you ask the question. And, you won't be distracted by a bunch of heads turning around to stare at you as you ask your question.

Don't wait. Ask your questions as soon as the professor has finished their thought. Taking this approach will help ensure that your question is answered fully and not cut short by the end of class.

Some of your lecture classes might not allow you to ask questions. If this is the case, make sure to write your questions down. Make sure you do this immediately while the question is fresh in your mind. Some professors may allocate time for questions at the end of the lecture; still, other courses may have small group meetings once a week to clarify any questions you have; still, others may require you to submit your questions via email.

Asking good questions is a skill, and the key to developing that skill is learning how to ask specific questions. "I don't understand" is a statement; it is not a question and drives professors nuts.

You need to provide your professor with some guidance about what you are having trouble with. "Can you clarify the difference between the 1st derivative and the second derivative?" is a much better way of asking for help as opposed to saying I am lost with this whole derivative thing.

If you have to wait until the end of the lecture to ask questions, give the professor some context for your question by referring to the part of the lecture that initiated the question. For example, "Professor, you said that during a digital marketing campaign, you will need to understand the noise in the communication channel. How would that differ, if at all, in offline channels?

Don't ask questions just to ask questions. If your question has not been well thought out, or the answer appears in your syllabus, or worse yet, the professor answered that question 15 minutes ago when you were on Instagram, you are just going to annoy the professor. And don't ask a question to try to look smart; professors are hip to that game and will see right through it!

Sometimes we struggle to get our actual points across, and we need to be careful in our communications not to send what is called "mixed messages" to others. A mixed message in this context is when the actual words being spoken are not consistent with the speaker's voice inflections and/or body language. This confuses others and makes them unsure of what the real message was supposed to be received.

You may experience mixed signals when dating, on the job, eating out, or even in the classroom. Your professor may say they are happy to help, but they did not look you in the eyes, they would not smile, shrugged, and their voice inflection seemed quite bothered. You now have experienced a clear, mixed message.

Maybe you asked your roommate how she was doing, and she said "fine" abruptly, short, and with very deflated body language. You just received another mixed message. Mixed messages are all around us, and we must pay attention to the communicator's vocabulary, voice inflections, and non-verbal behaviors to truly understand the message. When you find yourself in a situation where you are receiving a mixed message, remember the following concepts:

Don't jump to conclusions or assume anything. We all at times read into things, but we really don't know what is going on inside the head of anyone else.

Don't take it personally. Mixed signals may not have anything to do with you, people have a lot going on these days, and sometimes people are just having a really bad day, so resist the urge to take it personally.

Make sure you're not contributing to the problem. Be aware of your own emotions and feelings that may cause you to send your own mixed signals.

And finally, ask direct questions. Don't be confrontational or pushy. Ask a few clarifying questions. A few well-chosen questions can clear things right up. Sometimes you may need to just let some time pass and then reengage the conversation or just let it go altogether.

When it comes to our listening skills, we can make a general characterization of what is called soft and hard listening skills.

We would engage our soft listening skills when we are listening to chit-chat and listening to idle conversation, or just generally hanging out. We engage our hard-listening skills when we are listening to someone trying to inform or persuade us. Situations where we must evaluate things, analyze things, and make decisions based on the information being conveyed to us. These situations all require a higher level and a more engaged level of listening. When it comes to listening, there are actually seven levels of listening.

1. Not Listening: Not paying any attention to or simply ignoring the other person's communications.
2. Pretending to Listen: Acting like or giving the impression that you are paying attention to another person's communications, but in all actuality, you're not really paying attention to that individual. College students are experts in this one!
3. Partial Listening: Only focusing partially on the other person's communication and not giving it your undivided attention.
4. Focused Listening: This is the act of giving the person you are communicating with your undivided attention.
5. Interpretive Listening: It goes beyond just paying attention, and we are focused on trying to understand what the other person is communicating.
6. Interactive Listening: Being involved in the communication by asking clarifying questions or acknowledging understanding of the communication.
7. Engaged Listening: Requires our full and total engagement in our communications. It involves listening to the other person's words and feelings. We go beyond what were are hearing and seeing to make interpretations concerning the communication and sharing yours as well with the other person(s). In engaged listening, all parties are given the opportunity to fully express their views, feelings, and ideas.

There are some common barriers to effective listening you need to be aware of. The first barrier I want to discuss is our habits. Most of us don't listen to understand; we listen to respond! Way too often, we are worried about our response, what we are going to say, our comeback to someone else's statement.

It takes time and practice to actively listen and fully engage in the process. The next barrier I want to talk about is physiological barriers. Physiological barriers can include things like hearing problems, but with students, it is most often the rapid thought process that creates the obstacles.

Listeners typically process words at a rate of about 500 words per minute, while most speakers talk around 125 words per minute. This gap leaves us with a great deal of mental spare time to get distracted. Our thoughts drift, and it becomes very hard to pay attention to what is being communicated. This processing gap is one of the reasons effective listening takes so much work, patience, and practice.

Environmental barriers are all over campus. Let's face it, college dorms can be more like the club than the library, and college campuses are filled with noises of all kinds. Environmental noise is one of the most significant barriers to effective communication because it is so distracting, making it difficult or even impossible for people to hear what is being communicated.

Another significant environmental barrier is temperature. If the temperature in a location is too hot or too cold, it impacts how you communicate. It also impacts how you feel emotionally. People can become frustrated and angry when they are uncomfortable.

The place where communication takes place can also be another environmental barrier. Trying to study in Starbucks with others can be challenging if there are too many people intent on having a loud conversation, all this can lead to altered communication.

Other problems, such as bad lighting, uncomfortable chairs, too many people coming and going, can all distract students and take away from effectively communicating.

Attitudinal barriers are behaviors or perceptions that prevent people from effectively communicating. Our attitudes are formed based on our experiences, which help create our opinions, biases, and personal feelings.

Think about this, when is the last time you changed your opinion on a topic, a person, or an activity? It is extremely difficult to alter our own attitudes, never mind those of other people.

Attitudinal barriers arise from our own unique points of view or frame of reference, which is the sum of our beliefs, our experiences, hopes, fears, and expectations. A person's point of reference consists of personal, professional, and educational components, any or all of which can filter, distort, or block information and result in selective attention to information being communicated.

If the message being communicated is aligned with your own opinions and attitudes, you receive it favorably. Conversely, if the communication is not aligned with your views or seems to run contrary to your accepted beliefs, you are more likely not to receive or respond openly.

From an academic perspective, there are two main causes of attitudinal barriers:

The first is Egocentrism, which is an attitudinal barrier where we tend to be "self-focused" with the belief that our own ideas are more important or valuable than those of other people. This attitude is very annoying to other people and damaging to relationships as it tends to alienate egocentrics from those around them.

The next barrier is called a Judgmental attitude. A significant number of communication problems occur because our message must first pass through a judgment filter. As such, your message is not received based on the sender's intentions alone. This is why sayings like, "don't let the facts get in the way of your argument" have become so popular.

One thing I encourage all my students to do is talk to siblings or friends that have interests totally different than their own. Watch a podcast on topics that are new to you or don't even seem interesting

174

to you. The goal with all this is to gain new vantage points. These new vantage points will help you expand your filter set, reduce your biases, and be more open to contrasting views and opinions.

Another barrier to effective listening is our false assumptions. We believe listening comes naturally and requires no work on our part or that it is the sender's responsibility to effectively communicate. We often believe that talking has more advantages than listening. Other times we may feel like we have to win a debate instead of focusing on understanding the message that is being communicated.

Our culture gives us a unique way of seeing the world and plays a significant role in how we see life. Culture is something that is passed down from generation to generation.

Cultural diversity may create a communication challenges as the mindset of people from different cultures varies; the language, signs, and symbols can be different. Different cultures can have different meanings for words, slang, behaviors, and gestures. Culture also gives rise to implicit prejudices, behaviors, and opinions.

When communicating with individuals from different cultures, it is especially important not to be judgmental, to listen, to understand, not to respond, and to actively listen.

While students realize there are different learning styles, they are often shocked to learn that people listen differently. This is a key concept to understand because once we understand someone's listening style, we can adjust how we communicate with them, and as a result, our communication is more effective, more persuasive, and more likely to pass through the receiver's filters as intended.

There are four listening styles: Relational Listening, Analytical Listening, Task-Oriented Listening, and Critical Listening.

Relational Listening

Relational listeners are most concerned with their ability to emotionally connect with other people. They listen to understand how people feel, are aware of their emotions, and are highly responsive to those individuals. They are usually nonjudgmental.

One of the key benefits of relational listeners is that people getting "listened to" are more satisfied with relationships and life. People tend to feel more connected with you and more understood. Like with all styles, there are some drawbacks, and relational listeners often become overly involved with other's feelings and even internalize and adopt them. They can lose sight of the quality of information being given because they are emotionally vested. They can often be perceived as overly expressive.

Analytical Listening

Analytical listeners are most concerned about receiving the full message before coming to judgment. They want to hear details and analyze an issue from a variety of perspectives. They want to get as many facts and details as possible. Because of this approach, a key strength of analytical listeners is their ability to thoroughly access the quality of ideas. On the flip side, a key drawback is that their decision-making process is very time consuming, and they can be slow to make the required decisions.

Task-Oriented Listening

Task-oriented listeners are more interested in getting the job done. Efficiency is their goal. They expect people to make their points quickly and stay on topic. As such, efficiency is a key strength. However, a key drawback to this style is they are often very impatient individuals, which can strain relationships as these individuals are generally not good at responding with appropriate empathy. Task-oriented listeners can also be impulsive and struggle with thoughtful deliberation.

Critical Listening

Critical listeners have a strong desire to evaluate messages. They focus on the quality, accuracy, and consistency of the message. They are quick to point out that that action movie actor has shot their gun 36 times without reloading! A key drawback is these listeners are often perceived as nit-picky and annoying. On the flip side, a key strength is their ability to investigate problems and issues as well as ensuring compliance with rules and regulations.

Becoming a Good Communicator

Research has revealed that everyone has default styles of listening. When we understand the strength, weaknesses, and preferences of our own listening skills as well as those of others, we can drastically improve the quality of our communications.

If you want to become a good communicator, it all starts with being a good listener. We spend the majority of our time in some form of communication, and estimates are that we spend between 70% and 80% of our time communicating, and well over half of that time is spent listening. If you're like most students, you probably did not give much thought to the process of listening in high school.

Listening is not only one of the most important skills you can develop in college, but in life as well. Your ability to effectively listen has a major impact on your college GPA, job effectiveness, and the quality of your relationships you develop and maintain with other people.

When you become a skilled listener, your academic performance improves, as well as your ability to influence, persuade, and negotiate with others. You will have less conflict in your life, and you will have

177

fewer misunderstandings with your college classmates, your family, and your friends. And of course, all of these skills are fundamental to your future career success!

Active listening is the key to developing your world-class listening skills. The entire process of active listening requires you to make a concerted effort to deeply understand the entire message that is being communicated. This is not an easy process and requires a high level of mental engagement.

You have to learn to block out distractions around you. You must learn to listen to understand and not just to respond. You have to be focused and not allow yourself to drift off or let your mind wander.

You want to let the person who is speaking know that you understand what they are communicating. You can nod your head in agreement. Smile or a simple say "yes," "I understand," or "uh-huh." You are not necessarily agreeing with what is being said; you simply are just acknowledging that you are listening.

Most people want to hurry up and get their words in; they want to find a break in the action and jump right in. But you really want to respond in ways that will keep the other person talking. When they are talking, you are gaining information that you can use to persuade, motivate, or even close a deal. You can achieve this objective by asking clarifying questions or probing questions or interjecting a comment to direct the conversation.

So how can we become a more effective listener? Let's look at five key active listening techniques you can use to become a much more effective listener.

<u>Work on Paying Attention</u>

The first thing you want to do is work on paying attention. You need to work on giving the speaker your full attention and make sure you are acknowledging the message you are receiving. A few key tips here are to: Make and maintain eye contact. Clear your mind of other thoughts. Listen so can understand, not to respond! And don't get distracted by environmental factors.

Demonstrate You're Listening

Next, you want to demonstrate that you're listening. Use body language and gestures to show you are engaged. Nod, smile, and use your facial expressions. Maintain an open and welcoming posture. Encourage the person you are speaking with to continue speaking with acknowledging comments like "yes," "I understand," and "uh-huh."

Provide Feedback

Next, you want to provide feedback. As I mentioned, our culture, filters, assumptions, judgments, and beliefs distort messages. When you are listening, your main objective is to understand what is being communicated. This can require deep reflection, asking questions, and perspective. By paraphrasing what is being said with phrases like "What I'm hearing you say is," and " It sounds like you are saying" are all great approaches to make sure you are aligned with the speaker. Another approach is to ask clarifying questions like, "What do you mean by...?" "Are you saying...?"

Defer Judgement

Another key strategy is to defer judgment. This is a very difficult and challenging thing to do for even the most well-intentioned listener. Personally, I have to continually work on not interrupting others. Interrupting others creates frustration for the speaker and can change the dynamics and flow of the speaker's message. Allow the speaker to finish their points before you ask any questions.

And finally, respond appropriately. At its core, active listening is about creating and demonstrating respect and understanding. You are demonstrating you are engaged in the conversation, you are gaining perspective, you are listening to understand, you are demonstrating engagement and acknowledging the speaker. You are responding with your thoughts and opinions in a respectful manner. In the end, it is all about treating the speaker the way you would want to be treated.

Listening Has a Big Impact on Our Lives

Listening doesn't just impact our grades and careers; it can impact our health. A growing amount of research is demonstrating how the things that we listen to can impact our mental, physical, and emotional well-being. In fact, listening can impact our health in several different ways.

It turns out that listening to complaining is actually bad for you. Listening to someone complain, gripe, or nag for 30 minutes or more can cause damage to the part of your brain that handles problem-solving skills. Complaining is an emotionally draining experience. It zaps your energy and changes your emotional outlook. Try your best to avoid those Negative Nancy's.

The right music may actually make you smarter! Playing music while you study can potentially improve your grades. Studies have shown that listening to classical music while studying has been linked to a 12% increase in math test grades.

What you listen to also impacts your stress levels. A number of studies have linked listening to music to lower cortisol levels. High levels of cortisol can wear down the brain's ability to function properly. Stress can kill brain cells and even reduce the size of the brain. Chronic stress can have a shrinking effect on the prefrontal cortex, the area of the brain responsible for memory and learning.

What you listen to can also impact your weight. Researchers have shown that listening to calming music while dining out at restaurants resulted in diners consuming 175 fewer calories. If you want to lose weight, listening to music while you eat may just do the trick.

Students and people, in general, don't realize they are not good listeners. Most of us have ears that hear quite well, but often, we have not acquired the necessary auditory processing skills, which would allow us to effectively perform true listening.

Our society is tied together by our systems of communication. This communication depends on both the spoken and written word, and the effectiveness of the spoken word depends not so much on how people speak but on how they listen. Ultimately, your success in college and in life will be driven by how well you listen.

Just about everybody believes that they are good listeners. As a result, very few people give much thought to their need to develop better listening skills. I hope after reading this book, you understand just how important listening is to your success in college and in life.

Presentation Skills

You will be required to do quite a number of presentations in college, and in some classes, it is not uncommon for 25% or more of your grade to be dependent on your class presentations. Many students really struggle with getting in front of the class and presenting. A big realization for students is to understand that most of the other students are as nervous as they are.

Mastering presentation skills is not just helpful in college, but it is critical to your success in most careers. In fact, a survey conducted and published in Forbes found that 70% of people say presentation skills are critical for career success. My guess is the other 30% just haven't figured out how important presentations are to their success.

A big part of the stress is not the presentation itself, but the fact you have to get up in front of a group of people. You may be surprised to learn that half the population has a fear of public speaking. It doesn't matter how big or small the group; many people struggle to give presentations.

In today's incredibly competitive workforce, you need to be able to effectively communicate your ideas and opinions to be successful. Poor presentation skills mean that you will fail to inspire your teams, products may not sell, entrepreneurs could fail to attract funding, and careers fail to advance. This really is a significant price to pay for neglecting a skill that anyone can develop with just a little work.

Communication and presentation skills are a part of each other. To be effective in your communication, you need presentation skills. Presentation skills help you to communicate more effectively and professionally with your audience, boss, team members, students, and professors.

If you want to ultimately be successful in your career, excellent communication skills will serve as a foundation for that success. With so many people having a real fear of public speaking, there is a big opportunity for you to differentiate yourself by developing a comfort with public communication and speaking. Your success in college and in your future career will be greatly dependent on you making effective communication a top priority. There are four key elements to all presentations: content, design, structure, and delivery.

The first thing you can do to reduce your stress and anxiety is to make sure that you learn the material that is the subject of your presentation. During my business communication class, the first presentation I have students do is a group presentation, so they can get used to being up in front of the class and not feel like all eyes are on them.

The second presentation I have them do is to tell the class a story. Any story, something that happened to them, something stupid a friend did, a highlight of a spring break trip, etc. The idea here is for them to be relaxed as they know their story and nobody else does, so they don't have to worry about forgetting a fact, or messing up details, etc. They can just free flow it. Any question they would receive will not require any study, just a simple recall of the experience. When you know your subject well, you can focus on engaging your audience, not trying to remember what you are going to say.

Not knowing your material does more than just make you uncomfortable; it leads to a lack of engagement with your audience. One of the most consistent issues I see is that students want to read their slides. The slides are not your presentation. You are! You talk with your audience, not to your slides. The slides are there just to aid you, keep you on track. You want to make eye contact with your audience, vary the cadence and sound of your voice, use gestures, and ask questions of your audience to keep them engaged.

With presentations, less is often more. For most presentations, you should follow the K.I.S.S principle, which stands for "Keep It Simple Silly." Too much information can bore your audience and throw off your timing. Keep your slides brief and to the point. Simplicity trumps complexity!

You want to pay close attention to your template design and utilize colors that will connect with your audience. School colors are often a good choice for your college presentations if your professor has not provided a specific format. Most companies will have an approved corporate template for their business presentations.

People need both eyes and ears to follow you, so don't blind them with a clash of bright colors. Dazzling slides tend to downplay their actual content. Your attempt to throw light on a topic may actually have the opposite effect.

Consistency not just in your message but in your design is important. It allows you to move your audience along with you in the direction you want them to move. Inconsistency in your design can be distracting to your audience; they may even start reading things into a design change that you never intended, completely derailing your presentation or message.

Make sure you review your class rubric for guidelines on font type and sizes. It is a best practice to avoid Comic Sans like the plague. You should also avoid fonts with running letters. It is typically best to use no more than two types of fonts in your presentations, one for your headlines and one for your content.

Pictures and graphs, much like the slides themselves, are only there to aid you. Use too many, and your audience will be distracted or confused and will just check out.

Each slide in your presentation should cover a certain aspect or topic. You don't want to combine multiple ideas on the same slide.

The audience will find it much easier to follow your thought process when you stick to one point.

Unless your audience is a grade school class, avoid using a lot of amination or special effects. And when you do use these tools, don't use a wide variety. Keep it simple and keep it within the theme, and you will be effective.

When giving your presentation in class, you will likely need to login to your email or school's LMS in order to give your presentation. Make sure you know your login and password, bring your presentation on a USB drive as a backup.

I can't tell you how many students struggle to log in or can't find where they stored their presentation. This just leads to frustration, stress, and embarrassment, all things that will negatively impact your state of mind and, ultimately, your presentation.

This Maya Angelou quote is one of my favorites, and when it comes to presentations and communications with people, it should be front and center in your mind.

"I've learned that people will forget what you said, people will forget what you did, but people will never forget how you made them feel."

There are many emotional connections you can make with your presentations. You can make people smile, frown, laugh, cry, get angry, scared, or a host of other emotions.

Whatever emotion you are striving for, make sure it relates to the topic you're presenting. One thing I have learned through the years is that most people make judgments about you based on how you make them feel, not on the words you say. Find a way to connect and watch your presentation reactions and grades soar.

When transitioning between parts of your presentation, you want to provide clear verbal and visual cues that you are making a transition. Orient your audience to where you are in your presentation progression. For this transition, I can say something like: "So that's a few of the basics when preparing for presentations, and now I will transition into the nitty-gritty." "So, with that said, let's dive right in and learn how you can present just like a pro!"

You want to practice your presentation enough times so you can appear natural, allowing you to engage the audience and not read the slides or present like a prerecorded robot. Remember, the audience is your focus, not your slides.

You are going to be given a time requirement as part of your presentation, so you want to be aware that you may speak faster or slower when you get nervous. In front of a group, this can drastically impact the amount of time you use in class versus your practice sessions. As you give more presentations, you will learn if you go faster or slower in front of an audience and then make adjustments naturally.

Most people speed up and go through their content more quickly when they are nervous or unprepared. Others start to ramble on and on and spend way too much time on insignificant supporting points. So, here are two pro tips to help you.

Have a few questions ready to ask the audience if you find you are moving too fast. Questions like "Have any of you ever had this happen to you?" "What would you do if you were in this situation?" Raise your hand if you have ever experienced XYZ. You can always have a friend in class on standby to ask a question or share a story to help you out. Pulling in the class can not only increase engagement but helps fill time.

The next thing you want to do is have a couple of stories that further highlight your points ready to go. These stories, if not used, have no impact on the presentation, but if you need them, they further support the point. Getting behind, you tell one story. If you need to fill the time, you add another.

When concluding your presentation, you want to employ language that clearly signals to your audience that you are concluding your talk. Finish with an audience-centric call to action that is urgent and easy to execute. And of course, end with a "*thank you.*"

Managing your nerves and anxiety levels is key to giving your best presentation possible. But here is the thing, don't fight the fear. Rather accept your fear. Getting yourself worked up by wondering if others will pick up on just how nervous you are will only increase your levels of anxiety. Nerves aren't all that bad; you just need to learn to harness that nervous energy and transform it into positive enthusiasm, and you'll be well on your way to making an awesome presentation. Let look at a few things that can help you manage your nerves.

Take Deep Breaths

This is the go-to advice for nerves. When we're nervous, our muscles tighten up. You may even find yourself holding your breath. Don't do that! Go ahead and take a few deep breaths to get oxygen to your brain and relax your body.

Smile Often

The very act of smiling will release positive endorphins into your system. These endorphins will reduce your overall feelings of anxiety and balance your mood for the presentation. Smiling also exhibits confidence and enthusiasm to your audience. Make sure your smile is natural and not forced.

Positive Visualization

When we actively visualize a successful outcome in our minds, our brain is much more likely to align with those thoughts. With our thoughts and actions aligned, we improve our odds of a successful outcome. You don't have to be a "Zen Master" to use this tool. Study after study has proven the effectiveness of positive visualization. See yourself nailing the presentation as you practice your presentation and visualize your success as you get ready to perform your presentation to the class.

Arrive Early

Getting to your location early allows you plenty of time to get set up prior to giving your talk. Planning to arrive early builds in a buffer should there be traffic or an accident and ensures you won't be late. Of course, the extra time will allow you to get settled in and relax.

Transform Nervous Energy Into Positive Enthusiasm

Study after study has shown that an enthusiastic delivered speech can win out over even the most eloquent of ones. I make sure that I'm as enthusiastic and energetic as possible before giving a presentation.

Drink Water

You want to make sure you don't develop a dry mouth, which is a frequent symptom of stress and anxiety. You can prevent this by staying hydrated and drinking plenty of water before your talk (just don't forget to hit the bathroom before starting).

Practice

It goes without saying, you'll need to practice your presentation several times prior to giving it live. Practice is truly essential if you want to deliver an inspiring presentation. Record your presentation and play it back to evaluate areas where you need work. You can identify your filler words. A filler word is a meaningless word, phrase, or sound that marks a pause or hesitation in your speaking. Some of the common filler words are um, uh, er, ah, like, okay, right, and you know.

Your voice, how you project, where you use emphasis, and pacing are all critical skills to a well delivered and received presentation. Monotone presentations will put your audience to sleep.

Tips To Nail Your Presentation

Slow Down

First, make a concise effort to slow down. When we feel stress or the pressure is on, most of us tend to speak faster. When you speak too quickly, you may fall over your words and appear nervous and miss your time threshold from your presentation rubric.

Adjust Your Volume

Pay attention to the size of the room you are in and adjust your volume accordingly. When I was young, my mom and dad always told me to speak loudly and clearly. I never realize how important this advice was until I started giving large presentations. Always make sure to speak loud enough for everyone in the back of the room to hear you. Speaking in the proper volume for the room projects confidence and authority.

Fine-Tune Your Pitch

Pitch is the high or low notes you hit during your presentation or a conversation. High-pitched voices can be annoying and can come across as very squeaky. On the other hand, low-pitched voices can communicate authority. One of the real keys to delivering a great presentation is to vary the pitch of your voice. For instance, when asking a question, end the question with a higher pitch. When you make a statement, you could punctuate it with a lower pitch. Practice varying your pitch until it flows naturally and requires little thought on your part.

Smooth Your Tempo

The overall rhythm of your words should be steady. Increase the tempo or pace of your speech to convey action or excitement. Slow down purposefully to emphasize a word or phrase.

Pause When It's Appropriate

Pause briefly before and after you make an important point or transition between ideas. This allows you to create suspense and allow others to process your comments and fully absorb what you're saying.

Regulate The Emotion of Your Voice

Your emotion should match what you are saying and what you want your audience to feel. As you refine your ability to effectively use your voice, you'll be able to apply it to all areas of your life.

A General Outline For Your Next Presentation

When you are doing a presentation, whether in college or the professional world, you always have a goal. In college, the goal is to get a good grade, but your assignment will come with a goal, and you want to make sure your presentation type is aligned to properly get your message across. Follow this general outline when giving a presentation:

- Welcome your audience and introduce yourself.
- Capture their attention with a fact, a question, or use of humor if appropriate.
- Identify your number one goal or topic of the presentation.
- Give a quick outline of your presentation.
- Provide instructions for how to ask questions – Do you want them to raise their hand, wait to the end, etc.

We can typically categorize your presentations into six different goal-based or overall types of presentations. Throughout your college career, your professors will challenge you with different types of presentations; for the most part, your assignments will focus on two types. These two types of presentations are the informative presentation and the persuasive presentation, but I will cover the six primary presentations you will likely encounter.

Inform/Reporting

Most of the presentations in your career will be about informing the people. A client or boss may ask you to come and present an update on a project you are leading. Your audience is looking to be informed on the status. Are we on track? Behind schedule? Ahead of schedule? How are we doing on the budget? Are your milestones on track, etc.? They aren't looking for inspiration or humor. What people want with this type of presentation is a truly clear explanation of the status of the project.

Other typical presentations in this category would be things like conveying financial results or presenting findings of your research. You may need to inform a committee or support departments on the status of various activities. These types of presentations are often short and to the point. The goal here is to give the audience the key details and facts.

To Educate

Presentations become a bit more complicated when they aren't only to inform but are designed to educate. The goal is to have the audience come away with an understanding of what you have presented. They need to leave knowing more than a status.

The goal is for your audience to learn, so you need to teach or instruct the group of people in front of you. This means you need to be well versed in your topic. There are many different examples of this type of presentation. A workshop or training session is one example. Instructing your fraternity or sorority on new policies is another example.

Presentations to educate often will take you longer. These types of presentations will use more examples and go more in-depth. Often, these presentations are much more interactive since interaction helps improve learning.

Persuasive Presentations

The goal of any persuasive presentation is to influence a change in the belief, attitude, or behavior of another person. As an example, a persuasive presentation would not only inform the audience members about the benefits of your Instagram marketing but would also try to persuade them to hire you to manage their Instagram account.

To Activate

Close to persuasion is activation. These presentations introduce the audience to information that will make them move to take action. Charity fundraising presentations are incredibly good representations, but another example is the political speech. Politicians want people to vote for them or support a particular cause or to take a particular action. Or vice versa, people may want their politicians to take a specific course of action.

To get this sort of presentation to work, one of the most important ingredients is to tell the audience what you want them to actually do. If your audience doesn't know what you want them to do, why would they take any action? Another important ingredient is passion. When you are trying to make people move, they will only do that if they feel your passion.

To Inspire and or Motivate

There are certainly a lot of different emotions we feel as humans, but inspiration is one of the most motivating emotions we feel. For generations, great leaders have relied on their ability to inspire people to take action, adopt a certain belief, or change their behavior.

One great place to see these types of presentations is at a TED Conference. Most often, you see them at events aimed at personal improvement. You can also see the use of motivational speeches within businesses when management is trying to inspire the staff to work harder or get behind a new initiative or product. Some of the best motivational speeches you will find are in sports locker rooms when coaches are trying to get their teams out on the field full of positive adrenaline.

Talks that are the most inspiring are often very personal in nature. Overcoming hardship and achieving success are very commonplace themes. But it doesn't always have to follow overcoming a hardship. They can utilize what is called future casting, painting a picture of a wonderful future if the audience follows your advice. If they follow your advice, they will have more money, healthier environment, less stress, more happiness, and so on.

<u>To Entertain</u>

Most everybody enjoys being entertained. And one great way of entertaining people is to give a great presentation. Many of these kinds of presentations are done in intimate settings. For example, when you are entertaining guests in your home. Or even when you are doing a speech at someone's wedding or special occasion. But you can see these entertaining speeches in many other places. Examples include standup comedy, theatre, and also presentations at event openings. These are all examples of presentations that are meant to entertain. To make the audience laugh and feel happy.

To make this presentation effective, you have to give the audience what they are looking for: a good feeling. In order to make people feel good, you need to understand who is in the audience and what makes them tick. You need to do your research and deliver a presentation that hits the mark!

Organizing Your Presentation

Now that we have gone over the six most common types of presentations, let's look at how to organize your presentation. To properly organize your presentation, you must first decide if you are going to deliver a story-driven or premise driven presentation.

A premise driven presentation is based on a statement or idea taken to be true and on which an argument or reasoning will be presented to support the position. A politician may start with the premise that cutting taxes will drive economic growth and then follow the premise with facts and figures to support that position.

Stories are extremely powerful and can help you make emotional connections, simplify complex ideas, create memorable moments, and drive people to action. Stories typically follow a traditional three-act structure: Act I – The setup and plot point one. Act II – The confrontation and plot point Two. Act III – Resolution: pre-climax, climax, and finale.

Regardless of the type of presentation you are doing, there are three principles you should follow. I say principles because there is no cookie-cutter approach for every situation. You can adjust your presentation based on your situation and objectives. Let's start with focus.

The key to a great presentation is the focus of the presentation. Don't jump all over the place, don't use a bunch of random examples, don't make your point so complex nobody knows what the heck your point is. Don't keep piling on point after point causing your listener to wonder what it is you are even talking about. Stay focused!

Next, we have contrast. We understand facts when we can contrast them with other facts. We understand light when we compare it to darkness. Up versus down, tall vs. short, big vs. small. If we were to say that 30,000 prescriptions were written for opioids in small-town, USA last year, we have nothing to compare that to. But if I add that this is 3,000 prescriptions for every man, woman, and child in a small-town, USA. I now have a contrast that immediately says to me, something is wrong there! How can that be!

New ideas or products can be compared to old products or ways of doing things to demonstrate innovation, convenience, or ease of use. Think microwave oven versus the conventional oven, the cell phone vs. a landline. We can also compare current states to future states. When you use our diet plan, you will lose x pounds, be able to enjoy more energy, sleep better, have a better social life, and so on. Contrasts are extremely powerful!

Finally, we have the concept of unity in our presentation. Unity is extremely important in persuasion, action, and all other forms of presentations. Unity keeps your audience moving down the path you want them to go without getting sidetracked. Inconsistency can create doubt, uncertainty, an unwillingness to commit.

Now, principles are easy, but applying them can be hard. Ideally, your presentation should have one goal, one clear message that is supported by 3-5 key points. Make sure your slides make one point, and the images, text, and comments support this one point.

Have you ever watched a movie that kept moving back in forth in time? They quickly flash on the screen eight months earlier, or three years earlier, or two months ago. You quickly start thinking, wait, is that eight months earlier from three years ago or two months ago? Or maybe you missed the moment on the screen when they even transported you back a few months, and you are completely lost!

As a presenter, it is your job to make sure your audience is with you, that your presentation is clear and easy to follow. Don't jump around from point to point, and make sure to follow a clear story arc.

Your presentation must describe both problems and solutions; otherwise, it's pointless. If you take me on a journey, you identify a huge problem in the world, and you have moved me to action, I want to help. But then you say, I have no idea how we can fix all this! What was the point?

It is said a picture is worth a thousand words; if that is true, a contrasting set of pictures is worth 10,000 words. Showing things changing is a powerful tool in having your message stick with the audience.

Engaging your audience is key to an extraordinarily successful presentation. Asking questions pulls people in. This can be a simple as saying. Can I tell you a story? These five simple words will pull your audience back in; they will stop being distracted as they tune in to hear your story. Simple questions like... Are you guys following me? Is this making sense? Have you ever felt the same way? These types of questions draw people back into your presentation.

The S-Curve

The S-curve is a classic pattern of change and engagement. How can you take your audience on an adventure? You can follow a traditional format for telling a good story.

1. Context

Begin your story with a bit of background. Here's where you will establish the setting, introduce the central character or topic, and outline some basic details to provide context for the presentation.

2. Problem/Conflict

Conflict is a crucial element in a good story-based presentation. The presentation begins to take shape when you introduce a problem, conflict, or obstacle.

3. Solution

This is the turning point of the story. The narrative is the most exciting or intense, and the problem starts to be solved.

4. Call For Action

Once the climax has been achieved, and the problem is resolved, it's time for the call to action. What specific steps do you want your audience to take? Be clear and specific in your call to action.

5. Conclusion

End your presentation by thanking the audience and providing a clear call to action.

Some Final Thoughts On Presentations

Non-verbal communication is communicating without the use of any words. It includes facial expressions, eyes, touching, and tone of voice, as well as less obvious messages such as dress, posture, and spatial distance. Let's look at some helpful tips for using nonverbal communication to improve your presentation skills.

Eye Contact

Eye contact helps you demonstrate your interest in your audience. It also increases your perceived credibility. When you make eye contact with your audience, your chances of getting your message across goes up significantly. Making eye contact helps you establish a connection and bond with the audience. When you make eye contact with people while you are speaking, you build one to one bonds with them. It provides the foundation for creating a conversation with the audience.

Smiles Are Powerful

Smiling is one of the key things that will make you appear more likable and friendly to others. When you smile a lot, people see you as happy. People are much more receptive to happy people. People seem to be drawn to people who smile a lot. It has been said that when you smile, your audience will smile with you. And a smiling audience is a receptive audience. Smiling will help you get your points across and past your audience's filters.

Gestures

Gestures are another important form of nonverbal communication. But you must be incredibly careful with gestures to make sure they are natural and not distracting. Avoid choppy, sudden gestures when you're presenting. Make sure your hands are not in your pockets, you're not swaying back and forth or fidgeting with your body gestures. Focus on making your gestures smooth and fluid.

Posture And Body Orientation

Make sure to stand up straight and look directly at your audience. Move toward your audience to engage them; just don't stand in one spot. Spend most of your time facing the audience. If you're using slides, speak to the audience, not the slides. It's ok to look at a slide briefly, especially if you want to draw the audience's attention to it, but always turn back to the audience after a few seconds.

Proximity

I recommend you use a wireless device to advance your slides, as you don't want to be tied to the computer. This allows you to walk around the room, having a conversation with your audience, not talking at them from behind a computer. The closer you can get to the audience, the more attention they will naturally pay to what you are saying.

The more you practice these skills, the more proficient you will become. Great presentation skills are not beyond your reach; you just need to practice what you have learned here.

Conclusion

Being successful in college is not difficult, but it does take hard work, discipline, commitment, and a solid plan. It all starts with creating a clear vision for your life, committing to the process, and establishing goals to keep you on track.

In this book, I have focused on the transition and academic skills you need to be successful in college; these are the same skills that will serve you well in your life. When you take complete ownership and accountability in your life, you stop accepting excuses, stop doing the minimum to get by, and start striving to be the best version of yourself each and every day.

You recognize that everything you do is an important step toward your ultimate goal, and your character will not let you do anything but your best. You see, everything in life is a choice! Your results in your life are the sum of the decisions you make and the repeated actions taken or not taken compounded over time. While you're young, bad decisions, procrastination, inaction, and lack of focus have not had enough time to derail you. The compound effect of these decisions is contained due to the short period of time you have been on this planet.

If you goofed off in high school, no big deal. Well, I didn't get into the college I wanted, but this other college accepted me, no big deal. I didn't get the best grades in college, but hey, I did get my degree, no big deal. I didn't get hired at that amazing company, but I did get hired by a company, no big deal. I have news for you, it is a big deal, and one day you will look back and wish you had made a little bit more effort in life.

I hope that you will be one of the 20% of the population that enjoys their job and enjoys what they are doing. My hope for you is that you will use the tools in this book to provide a foundation not just for your academic success but a successful and fulfilling life!

The choice is yours! You owe it to your future self to give it everything you have today! If you have made it to the end of this book, I know you are one of the 20 % of the people living their dreams every day!

I would love to hear from you on your journey. DM me on Instagram @DennisStemmle, or email me at Dennis@CollegeSuccessAcademy.com.

Please head over to www.GetMyFreeBookResources.com, as I have a few FREE gifts for you to help you get more out of this book faster! Go Make It Happen!

About The Author

Dennis Stemmle is the creative and driving force behind College Success Academy as its founder and Chief Evangelist. As a business leader and educator with over two decades of experience, Dennis brings a unique perspective that bridges the divide between the classroom and the "so-called" real world.

Dennis simply distills the best of the best information and strategies available for college success, mixing his street-tested principles with those of teachers and students from around the country. He is also a best-selling author, successful entrepreneur, speaker, and Lecturer in the Department of Management and Decision Science at Coastal Carolina University.

Follow Dennis on Instagram and Twitter @DennisStemmle and on Facebook @CollegeSuccessAcademy.

Visit Dennis online at CollegeSuccessAcademy.com and learn more ways you can be successful in college.

Online Companion Resources

This book comes with a FREE companion online digital training course. To claim this book's companion resources, please visit www.GetMyFreeBookResources.com and claim your training now.

Made in the USA
Las Vegas, NV
09 February 2023

67208957R00125